THE LOG CABIN

THE LOG CABIN

HOMES OF THE NORTH AMERICAN WILDERNESS

Text and drawings by Alex W. Bealer
Photographs by John O. Ellis

Barre Publishing

BARRE, MASSACHUSETTS

Distributed by Crown Publishers, Inc. New York

Contributing photographer for western and Canadian
log buildings: RONALD WOODALL

Frontispiece: The Slave Cabin at the Tullie Smith House Restoration
on the grounds of the Atlanta Historical Society.

Published simultaneously in Canada by General Publishing Company Limited

First edition

Printed in Japan by Dai Nippon Printing Co., Ltd., Tokyo

Library of Congress Cataloging in Publication Data

Bealer, Alex W
        The log cabin : homes of the North American wilderness.

        Bibliography: p.
        Includes index.
        1.   Log cabins—United States. 2.   Log cabins—Canada.
        1.   Ellis, John O., joint author.   II.   Title.
        NA8470.B35   1978   728'.7   77-26316
        ISBN 0-517-528924 (cloth)
        ISBN 0-517-533790 (paper)

10 9 8 7 6 5 4

Contents

PART ONE

THE LOG CABIN TRADITION

Beginnings

Front cover of campaign music for William Henry Harrison.

About the middle of the eighteenth century, when the English settlers in America began to spread out from the eastern seaboard into the vast uncharted forests of the West, the log cabin came into its own as a part of American legend.

In virtually every settlement there was a log cabin. For poorer families it was a residence that might last for generations. For those who were rich enough to own slaves or hire farm help, cabins were built to use as temporary homes during the years it took to build a permanent residence of brick or clapboard.

The log cabin was ubiquitous along the frontier because it was so eminently suitable to the environment. It could be made entirely of the logs that grew so plentifully and in such great variety in the American forest. Some of these logs were hewn and some were split into roof shingles. Even the chimney of a temporary cabin could be made of logs and clay, and many a frontier cabin was built without a single iron nail, iron hinge, or anything else made of iron.

Often a simple cabin was built with only two metal tools: the remarkable American ax, which was used to fell and buck the trees, hew them in rough squares, and cut the corner notches; and the simple, ancient froe that was needed to rive shingles or roof boards. Cabins built with these elementary tools could provide shelter and even comfort for several lifetimes, needing only a new roof every half century or so.

Despite its simplicity, however, the log cabin provided excellent shelter from the driving winds of winter and the drenching rains of spring, and at times from the arrows or bullets of savage enemies. Its thick logs with interstices chinked with clay or moss, its notched and fitted construction, its durable oak- or chestnut-shingled roof, made it both sturdy and cozy, albeit some were a little insect-prone in the summertime in the piney woods of the southern coastal plain.

Any man with a modicum of skill with an ax could build his own cabin in a relatively short time if he did not mind hard work. After a while the cabin's grayed horizontal logs blended in perfectly with the gray and black and brown vertical tree trunks of the mother forest, as the smoke from the fieldstone chimney melded with the limbs and branches.

In the generations from the beginning of the westward movement until the beginning of Republican/Democratic government, the log cabin became a symbol of the self-reliance, the courage, and the ingenuity of the American people. Because of this, from the first campaign of Andrew Jackson, who was the first of our presidents to be born in a log cabin, until the election of Abraham Lincoln, who was the last, the log cabin had great significance in American political history. By 1828, when Jackson was elected president, the frontier vote had become decisive in national politics. Frontier settlers, who had multiplied by millions as the new nation grew rapidly westward to the banks of the Mississippi River, were for the first time politically powerful enough to rebel against the large landowners of the East, the few remaining patroons of the Hudson River valley, the aristocratic planters of Virginia and South Carolina, and the wealthy merchants of New York, Boston, and Philadelphia. Jackson let the electorate know that he had been born under British rule in a log cabin on the South Carolina frontier, which made "Old Hickory" very popular with all those people then living in log cabins west of the Appalachians. They elected him president, twice.

General William Henry Harrison, "Old Tippecanoe," was no fool either. Despite the fact that he had been born in a tidewater Virginia mansion, he blatantly used the log cabin as his campaign symbol and won the presidency. Other candidates for national office also tried to woo the frontier vote by associating themselves with log cabins, whether or not they had been born and reared in one, and frequently that association did help get them elected.

Abraham Lincoln, father of the Homestead Act and a fine example of how a poor, uneducated boy from a nondescript family can rise to become president of the United States, was born and grew up in log cabin society. In his autobiography Lincoln is somewhat laconic about his early frontier years, but he does mention that as a boy and a young man he helped his father build several log cabins for the family in Kentucky and Indiana. During his political campaigns and his presidency Lincoln never

This cabin, from Knob Creek Farm in Kentucky, is a replica of one of several log cabins—in Kentucky, Indiana, and Illinois—in which Abraham Lincoln lived as a boy. During the five years the Lincoln family spent here, from 1811 to 1816, a younger son, Thomas, Jr., was born and died in infancy. Located on its original site south of Louisville in Hodgenville, Knob Creek Farm is open to the public. *Photograph courtesy the Kentucky Department of Public Information*

Davy Crockett of Tennessee, a hero in both folklore and history, was another prominent American who lived virtually all his life in log cabins. One of these houses was the log tavern built in 1794 and operated by Crockett's father, John, near Morristown, Tennessee. David lived here from 1794, his eighth year, until 1798. The Crockett Tavern consists of a nicely fitted story-and-a-half pen with a Tennessee limestone chimney. This is expanded with a one-story log wing that has its own chimney and probably was used as the kitchen. On a slope behind the tavern is a lean-to that served as storage space for wagons and other equipment. Although the paneled shutters on the front windows might seem to be an affectation of the restorers, it is quite possible that a well-made log building of the period and location of the Crockett Tavern would have boasted such refinement. *Photograph courtesy Tennessee Department of Tourist Development*

made much of his frontier background; but this background was well known to the electorate of his day, and there is little doubt that it helped to elect him.

So durable was the symbolism of the log cabin in our political history that Senator Robert Kerr of Oklahoma, who had brief presidential aspirations during the 1950s, proudly advertised that he had been born in a log cabin in his native state.

It is not surprising, then, that Americans and other peoples of the world alike look upon the log cabin as a peculiarly American phenomenon. They think that the log cabin sprang up in the New World because of need and then spread like pine saplings in a deserted field throughout the vast reaches of virgin forests that lay between the eastern seaboard and the edges of the Great Plains.

But this is a romantic fallacy, pleasant and inspiring but quite erroneous. The log cabin, like the American people, had its origin in Europe. And like the American people, that potpourri of cultures faced with the problems of survival in a wilderness, the log cabin was adapted to American conditions and served its function well.

Indeed, the log cabin in America was an echo of the distant, prehistoric past, from a part of Europe where ancient conditions were quite similar to those of the wilderness in the New World. All signs point to the fact that the log cabin was originally conceived in prehistoric Scandinavia and the Baltic countries, an area that once boasted woods as vast and mysterious and inviting as the American forest. It was brought to America by Scandinavians, fortuitously, at a time when the ease of its basic design and construction were needed to help transform with relative speed the frontier of the American colonies into prosperous settlements.

Most accounts agree that America got the log cabin from those pioneering Swedes who settled the first and last Scandinavian colony on the continent, New Sweden, in 1638.

The Swedish settlers were better prepared to cope with the problem of housing in a forested wilderness than settlers from most other nations in the world at that time. For in Sweden, and other areas of Scandinavia, the log cabin had been part of the culture since prehistoric times when certain tribes were driven out of northern Germany across the Skagerrak into the pristine forests of the Nordic peninsula. There they invented the

Facing page:

Skansen in Stockholm, Sweden, is a remarkable outdoor museum of Swedish building history. It includes the farmstead from Mora, or Moragården, which was moved to the park and restored in 1895. Most of the structures in this complex were built between 1574 and 1595 and lived in until almost 1895. The log storehouse shown on the facing page, top far left, is said to date from the fourteenth or fifteenth century. Apparently its weathered wall logs are oak. The traditional roof is made of planks, with birch bark laid between the two courses of the planks. The storehouse's construction does not differ markedly from the typical American log cabins that were built in the backwoods so plentifully during the eighteenth and nineteenth centuries. One distinction, however, shown in the middle picture, is the inverted saddle notching of the corners. In cabins built subsequently in Sweden and America, the notches were cut on the bottom of the logs; this ancient structure has its notches cut on the top of each log. Certainly, this method would allow each notch to be cut accurately after the log was put in place, probably saving a great deal of time. However, inverted notches tended to collect rainwater and snow, hastening the rotting of the structure's corners.

The top right photograph is of an eighteenth-century log farmhouse from Oktorp, moved and restored at Skansen, which exhibits a typically Swedish corner fireplace. This kind of fireplace, which could be found in the earliest cabins built by seventeenth-century Swedish settlers in America, was replaced by conventional chimneys in later American log cabins.

The remarkable octagonal log windmill shown in the bottom left picture dates from the seventeenth century and has been restored behind the Småland Museet at Växjö in Sweden.

The farmhouse in the bottom right photograph is from Kyrkbult in southern Sweden and has been restored at Skansen; its age has not been determined. However, historical documents tell us that low, turfroofed domiciles set closely between tall storehouses were widely used in this district during the Middle Ages. This rather comfortable cottage has a corner fireplace for heating and cooking, but its skylight is a vestige of the old smoke holes of Viking times, before chimneys were adopted in the northern countries.

construction technique of the log cabin: horizontal logs laid in courses with notched and fitted corners that locked the whole into a stable, hollow mass in which men and animals could live.

Such a design was perfect for the environment of New Sweden and its capital, Fort Christina. The colony was quickly established and prospered despite a lack of communication with, and general neglect from, the mother country, then embroiled in military and political problems.

Things became worse when Christina, for whom the capital had been named, gained the throne in 1644. She was a willful, rebellious, misanthropic young lady who affected men's clothes, refused to marry and produce an heir to the throne, and bitterly fought the domination of men in her court and the influence of the Protestant state church. She recklessly expended crown funds on her favorites at court, and finally, the drama of the act appealing to her, abdicated her throne and became a Roman Catholic.

During her short but merry reign Christina gave little thought to the potential of New Sweden, and her behavior distracted others in her government from providing the colony with proper support and security. As a consequence, New Sweden was captured first by the Dutch in 1655 and later by the English in 1664, all of which shattered the integrity of the Swedish element in the colony. The colony eventually became Delaware, which was the first state to ratify the new Constitution of 1789 for the United States of America.

By 1664 settlers of Swedish descent, now colonial citizens of Britain with legal access to other British colonies, began to move westward into Pennsylvania and Maryland, taking their exemplary housing with them. Like their ancestors who went *a viking,* they moved into the wilderness, armed with farming implements and felling axes instead of the shields and swords of ancient times. No longer the adversaries of centuries before, the British and Swedish settlers migrated together, and the Swedes demonstrated the advantages of log cabin construction in their new settlements.

Since the British Isles had been invaded and deeply influenced by Viking hosts as early as A.D. 800, one may wonder why the British were ignorant of log cabin construction when they in turn invaded the forests of the New World. One can only surmise that in Anglo-Saxon Britain the Vikings brought new Scandinavian ideas to an already well-established culture. The cumulative influence of the brilliant achievements of Roman, Greek, Egyptian, and other ancient Mediterranean civilizations had created in King Alfred's England a stable society, with farms, towns, and churches, and an active commercial community. The England of that time had no need for log cabins. Conditions did not require them.

All was different in the pristine reaches of eastern North America. All was forest in America, infrequently interrupted by small clearings for Indian villages and gardens. And as the settlers from England, Scotland, Wales, and Ireland moved into new lands, they mingled with the Swedes from Delaware, all of them facing the same problems and using what they had, mainly themselves and their environment, to provide their families with food, clothing, and shelter. They shared the ideas needed for survival and progress.

Immigrants from Britain, of course, were not ignorant of the techniques of building houses. For generations, since the dawn of history in the Isles, farm people, serfs and yeomen alike, had been building houses and barns and other outbuildings from material found in their native land—stone and turf in most instances. Those who were better off built houses of timber and brick, some of half timber and wattling, the framework fitted together with mortise and tenon that matched ship construction in the precision of its joints. Richer families had the time and available help to spend several years building half-timber manor houses. And they could always stay with others in the family while their homes were being built.

In North America substantial shelter was needed immediately, for the winds of winter would not wait for a traditional house to be built, and there were no relatives in the wilderness with whom to stay during the years it took to build such a dwelling. There were few spots in the middle of the woods that would yield enough stones to build an English-type cot, and woodland turf was not suitable for building. Also, in most instances, there was no labor force available as in Britain, so a man and his family were dependent on themselves to build the shelter they needed.

True, in eighteenth-century Virginia and North Carolina some wealthy slaveholders carried their labor force with them to settle new lands, and on many occasions set the slaves to building temporary housing for the master to live in while a big brick house was being built, but again

In this picture, Swedish emigrants are constructing a log building near Swedes Lake, Minnesota, in 1856, the beginning of Swedish settlement of this area. *Photograph courtesy American Swedish Institute*

An abandoned log cabin that was built by Swedes in Minnesota. Date and location are unknown. *Photograph courtesy American Swedish Institute*

A Scotsman, Captain Basil Hall, Royal Navy, traveled extensively in the settled regions of North America in 1827–28, taking with him that innovative device, the camera lucida. Hall's camera lucida provided illustrations for his three-volume work, *Travels in North America*, and an accompanying volume entitled *Forty Etchings from the Camera Lucida*. One of these illustrations, "Log House in the Forests of Georgia," shown at top, is of a very rough cabin, which was apparently constructed of small, unhewn logs with a shake roof. The building is entirely without windows, and Captain Hall, who asked about this omission, reports that the cabin owner explained, ". . . we never make the windows in the first instance, but build up the walls with logs, and then cut out the windows. Now, I have not enough money to enable me to go into that matter; but I hope in the course of the year to put in a couple of glazed windows."

time was a factor. Fields had to be cleared so that there would be no loss of income, and the slaves themselves also needed houses. Livestock needed shelter, too.

The solution to all of these problems of shelter was apparent when British settlers were introduced directly or indirectly to the traditional Scandinavian log cabin. As the Swedes spread out from Delaware, and new British settlers came into the areas occupied by colonists of Swedish derivation and their descendants moved southward and westward, the log cabin, with its concomitant barns and smokehouses and shops of logs, was adopted over a couple of centuries by virtually the whole restless frontier. It was the construction that was adopted, however, rather than the floor plan of the Swedes. The cabins, or in some cases log houses, were designed by British settlers to follow the ancient plans of rural houses in England, Scotland, Ireland, and Wales. So, in time, the log cabin became a polyglot of cultures; it became American in every sense of the word.

Although log cabins did not provide the comfort and graceful living one found in manor houses of England, Scotland, and Sweden, they offered much more than the circular, mud-daubed, bark-roofed houses of the Indian tribes in America. The Indians, consequently, adopted the log cabin as readily as Scots and Englishmen, particularly in the Southeast, where the tribes enjoyed a longer tenure on their patrimonial lands and a longer association with white men.

No one knows exactly at what period Indians began to build themselves cabins like those of the encroaching white man, but it had to have been after they began to trade skins and furs for that essential tool in cabin building, the steel ax. The Creeks and Cherokees were trading with Spaniards as early as 1540, but these tribes could hardly have seen log cabins until the first half of the eighteenth century, when the Swedish influence in cabin building finally reached the southeastern frontier. One can speculate that cabins first appeared in the region when the colony of Georgia was established in 1733 to provide protection to South Carolina from the Spaniards in Florida, thus attracting new settlers from Europe and the northern colonies to the Carolinas as well as to Georgia.

There are a few Indian log cabins left. There is an example of a Cherokee cabin dated ca. 1760 in a park in Chattanooga, Tennessee. Also, in Westville, a restored village of the 1850s near Lumpkin, Georgia, there is a Creek Indian cabin of ca. 1820 that has been·preserved, altered, and finally restored to its original condition (see Part Two). On the Qualla Reservation of the Cherokees in the Smoky Mountains of North Carolina, cabins were built until the 1950s.

At first the Indians probably adopted only the basic construction, horizontal logs notched and fitted at the corners, and retained the Indian tradition of a small doorway, a roof of bark, and a smoke hole instead of a chimney. Actually, many of the abandoned cots of eighteenth-century emigrant Irish, English, and Scots had only smoke holes in the ancient tradition of Norse halls; the chimney was not known in western Europe before about the twelfth century, and many rural Britons were quite behind the times.

Indian cabins, until quite late in history, had dirt floors for the most part, and most probably retained the raised sleeping platforms that were typical of aboriginal houses. Probably the earliest Indian-built log cabins used round, unhewn logs, and many of the later ones were made of logs only very roughly hewn. The Welles House at Westville has the sophistication of a chimney and split shingles, but originally, as shown in the restoration, it had a dirt floor and evidence of a raised platform in front of the fireplace where its inhabitants slept and stored certain possessions in the old Creek manner.

Some Cherokees, however, during the late eighteenth and the nineteenth centuries built quite magnificent residences of squared logs. Soloman Owle had a beautiful two-story log house he built himself on Goose Creek in North Carolina in the 1890s. Unfortunately, it has now been replaced with a modern frame house, but in its time it provided a home place for a large family of Owles. Virtually all the Cherokees lived in log cabins in their native lands before their removal and in Arkansas and Oklahoma afterward, happy with the improvement in housing they had borrowed from the white man, never knowing that its origins lay in the forests of prehistoric Sweden.

At Ross' Landing, outside Chattanooga, Tennessee, there still stands the splendid two-story log house of John Ross, the wealthy, well-educated, and highly respected chief of the Cherokees at the time of the tribe's removal to the West. As it has been restored, the Ross House seems to have always had exposed logs in the tradition of the simple cabins that

An Indian cabin of the early 1800s near Atlanta, as reconstructed in a painting by the late artist and historian Wilbur G. Kurtz. Its chimney is made of logs protected from the flames of the fire by a clay lining. The notched and crossed poles on the roof illustrate one of the techniques for holding roof shakes in place without the use of nails.

On the Qualla Indian Reservation, adjacent to the Great Smoky Mountains National Park, Cherokees lived in log cabins until well after the tourist era began. The picture at right, taken in the 1930s, shows two log dwellings that were still in use then but have since been destroyed. Despite the severity of the winters in the North Carolina mountains, neither of the cabins shown is chinked. Both are protected from winter winds only by interior boarding, which did not furnish the insulation of clay chinking. The children are Cherokee.

The John Ross House at Rossville, Georgia, as it looked almost a century before it was partially restored as a two-story, dogtrot log cabin. This photograph was taken in 1864 immediately following the bloody battle of Chickamauga when the Ross House served as a general headquarters. Damage from the battle or neglect allows us a glimpse of the strong log pen beneath the clapboards, a frequent substitute for the mortised, tenoned, and pegged house frames common before 1840. This house, which is thought to have been built around 1790, served as the Cherokee chieftain's home until shortly before the Cherokee Nation was forcibly removed to Arkansas in 1838 and 1839.

expedited the settlement of the American West. Yet there is a photograph in *The Photographic History of the Civil War* (edited by Francis Trevelyan Miller and published by the Review of Reviews Company, New York, 1911) that shows the Ross House was covered with clapboards when photographed in 1864 at the time Chattanooga was captured by the Union Army. This, with the evidence of flat notched corners, indicates that the house was always intended to be weatherboarded and that its underlying log structure merely served as a frame for the weatherboarding. This point will be discussed more fully later in Chapter Four. So, as it stands today, the John Ross House is probably only partially restored. It may have seemed to the restorers that Indians, regardless of affluence or intellectual achievement, could live only in log cabins.

A word must be said also for the Russian and German tradition of living in log cabins, although emigrants from neither nation were present in numbers enough to affect the settlement of America prior to 1750. Actually, it could well be that Russians originally learned of log cabins from Swedes who invaded the vast, mysterious country to the east in Viking times. And it's quite probable that the northern Germans, who were exposed to the culture of the aggressive Swedes at an early date, learned to build log cabins from the same source.

One must not overlook either the contributions of the French to the tradition of log cabins as suitable wilderness dwellings. French emigrants came to North America early in the seventeenth century by a route quite different from those of the British and Swedish settlers. The French established themselves first in Canada and expanded southward from the Great Lakes along the Mississippi River and then eastward up the Ohio and Tennessee rivers to the Appalachian Barrier. They never reached the Atlantic coast and were evicted from Canada and the regions west of the

Appalachians when defeated in the War of Jenkins's Ear, better known in America as the French and Indian War. This eviction occurred in 1763 before there was any appreciable contact between French traders moving eastward and British and Swedish settlers moving westward from the Atlantic coast. Yet the French built log cabins, although the French structures were built differently from German, English, and Scotch-Irish cabins and somewhat differently from the cabins built by Swedes in the mid-seventeenth century.

By most standards it is difficult to see sophisticated Frenchmen, whose intellectual and scientific achievements were unsurpassed in all of Europe during the reigns of the Sun King and that of his heir in the late seventeenth century and through three-quarters of the eighteenth century, inventing during this time anything so relatively crude as a log cabin. What cultural tradition, if any, led the French to log cabin design, however different it may have been from the typical American log cabin of Andrew Jackson and William Henry Harrison?

There *is* a cultural source of French log cabins. Normandy was settled by Norsemen during the tenth century. Norsemen brought with them the tradition of the log cabin, and possibly that tradition flourished more in tenth-century France with its limited population and vast, variegated forests than it had in more settled England. Such a theory can be supported by the fact that French cabins, even those built in the nineteenth century, were constructed similarly to Scandinavian cabins and the cabins of the early Swedish settlers of Delaware, Pennsylvania, and New Jersey during the seventeenth century. This point will be explored more fully in Chapter Four. It gives strength, however, to the theory that the concept of horizontal timber construction undoubtedly originated in Scandinavia in prehistoric times.

In 1877 a surveyor and amateur photographer, David Carlisle Humphreys of Charlottesville, Virginia, joined a government expedition to survey the upper reaches of the Missouri River, a territory still threatened by attacks from Sioux, Cheyenne, and Arapaho warriors. While the wilderness of the plains country in the late nineteenth century provided a few more creature comforts than the forests of the East had offered its first settlers, the log cabin was still a favored form of building. Clearly a business establishment, the saloon at right reflects Scandinavian influence in line and structure, and well it might. More than a million Norwegians, Swedes, Finns, and Russians left rockbound farms in northern Europe to settle on free land in the United States during this period. The low gables exhibited by this building were no longer used in the East in the late nineteenth century. The logs in the main building are nicely hewn and fitted, and log purlins, for the most part abandoned two generations before in the East, here support a turf roof, still found at the time in Scandinavia. Little is known of the exact location or of the builders of this log structure, but its style could well reflect a neo-Scandinavian influence on housing in the West after the Civil War, some two hundred years after the first log cabins were built by the Swedish colony in Delaware. *Photograph courtesy Missouri Historical Society*

Another log dwelling on the upper Missouri in the late 1870s. The builder of this cabin was apparently able to claim land near a stream, which the presence of trees in the background suggests. The scene could have been duplicated in Finland or Sweden in the same period. *Photograph courtesy Missouri Historical Society*

Some sources mention the fact that early Swiss settlers also shared the tradition of log cabins. This may be true, but the proportion of eighteenth-century American pioneers from Switzerland was small indeed, and never concentrated as the Swedes and Germans were. Besides, most Swiss immigrants to America were of Germanic descent. It is doubtful that the Swiss had any deep influence on the widespread adoption of log buildings on the American frontier.

Those particularly interested in architecture may tend to look upon log buildings as being primitive and somewhat dull, reflecting little imagination. This is not true. American log cabins and houses were really expressions of folk art with roots in the dim past of the far northern forests. Each cabin had its own characteristics and character: varying widths of logs, different types of mud chinking depending on locality, interesting and unique roof textures created by the variations in individually hand-split shingles.

In addition, most log cabins and houses formed only one part of a cluster of buildings, the organization and numbers of buildings in each complex being dictated by need, topography, and convenience. Some had huge log barns consisting sometimes of four separated cribs, each as large as a normal cabin, all covered by a common shingled roof with extended eaves to provide storage for wagons, carts, and other farm equipment. Most had a corncrib, single or double, a chicken house, a pig house, all sturdily built to repel bears, cougars, foxes, and rats, and all usually built of that inexhaustible building material of the frontier, logs. Often there were additional log buildings for blacksmithing and woodworking shops. On every farm each outbuilding, like the residence, was fashioned to dimensions that fit available logs and the taste of the builder.

The Civil War, through which Abraham Lincoln led our country, was known to many in the South as "A rich man's war and a poor man's fight." For the most part the Confederate troops were farmers and backwoodsmen. When winter came and these troops were immobilized at Centreville, Virginia, they created their own snug quarters by building log huts, complete with stick-and-clay chimneys. This photograph was taken by Mathew Brady in 1862.

Far from being monotonous, log cabins and houses and concomitant structures actually formed sculptural groups of divergent elements and with diverse colors and textures. Exposed to the weather of all the seasons, each building soon assumed the soft lavender-gray of weathered wood, which was complemented by the wispy green of early spring, the brilliant oranges and yellows of autumn leaves, and the bare brown of tree trunks in wintertime. The logs and shingles were still trees but in another form, and the buildings fit appropriately into the landscape of early America, becoming a part of the rich, fruitful earth.

Sturdy and indestructible though they were, there was an ethereal quality also about such buildings. They appeared almost as visions from a distance, set solidly against a background of woods or fields. Approaching them on a frosty morning in fall, when the wood smoke from the stone chimney lay close to the hoary ground, one could sense the security, the coziness and protection offered in the simple room with the low blazing fire.

A frontier farm composed of log buildings might be likened to a medieval monastic complex on a hilltop in Italy, or the layout of a thirteenth-century castle spread along a ridge between two protective rivers, or an ancient Norse farmstead on the edge of a wilderness where aurochs roamed. Such farms were never entirely American. Such farms were an inheritance, a cultural relic from man's past in Europe.

There were many cabins, barns, corncribs, and other structures built of logs in America between about 1750 and 1950. One sometimes wonders what became of them all. Only a few are left today, and most of them are restored, which happily saves them for posterity but yet takes away from them the inexorable mystique found in a log building in use.

Back in the 1930s an applicant for a doctorate made a survey of log cabins in Georgia and wrote his dissertation on the findings. Among other things the survey found that at that time there were more than ten thousand log cabins still standing in the state, many of them still occupied. At that time, too, it is quite safe to guess that new log buildings were still being raised in the state, particularly in the isolated mountain areas, and in the whole area of Appalachia that stretched from Georgia into Pennsylvania. There were few paved roads in this stretch of mountains until after 1940, so if a man needed a dwelling for his family or a shed for his animals, he made them of logs as his father and grandfathers and great-grandfathers had done. It was too difficult to haul in heavy truckloads of lumber over roads hub-deep with mud in many areas, and, besides, it cost too much, and money was as scarce as sawmills.

A few people lived—and possibly some still do—in ancestral log cabins until the age of space exploration. An outstanding example of this disappearing, if not extinct, group was James F. Whitley of the upper settlement of Vinings, Georgia, now an affluent suburb of Atlanta. About 1960 Mr. Whitley was forced to move from the cabin in which he had been born in 1873 because of the construction of the perimeter highway around Atlanta. His grandfather had built the cabin in 1842, shortly after the Cherokees had been moved out of the state over the Trail of Tears to faraway Arkansas. Whitley grew up on the place, left for a few years to practice as a general blacksmith and as a railroad carpenter, then returned to his old home place in the 1920s. At that time he built himself a log barn and a log blacksmith shop and settled down to live the rest of his life as his father and grandfather had. Each spring he rechinked between the beautifully hand-hewn logs. When the roof began to leak in the late 1950s, he cut down his own white oak board tree, bucked it, split the logs into bolts, and from these rived new shingles, which could be counted upon to last at least fifty years. Note that this was in the 1950s, a couple of generations after the so-called demise of the American frontier. This cabin was a pure relic of the earlier days of self-sufficiency. It never had electricity, even after electricity was readily available. Its only compromise with modernity was a lean-to kitchen, added by Whitley himself, which contained a castiron, wood-burning stove. But as he grew older the venerable gentleman went back to cooking over the broad stone hearth

Jim Whitley at the treadle lathe he made himself. The squirrel rifle he is holding is a family heirloom.

where his mother and grandmother had cooked countless meals of venison and squirrel, passenger pigeon and quail, and home-grown vegetables, using the pothooks and the chimney bar that they had used.

Fortunately, despite the environmental destruction brought by the new expressway, the old Whitley cabin, itself an integral part of the environment, was moved and carefully restored, as much as it is possible to restore such a memento of the frontier (see the photographs of the cabin in Part Two). But yet it will never be the same, any more than will any other restored cabin. It is as difficult to transplant an old cabin as it is to move a white oak seedling from the forest. The true, undefinable spirit, or spirits, of the place have been lost, just as poltergeists are lost from old houses that undergo extensive alterations. It is now an example of what once was—not quite the actual thing.

It is not likely that the true American log cabin will be seen in quantity again because it is no longer needed. The old cabins were not just buildings of logs and clay and fieldstone chimneys; they were answers to a desperate need, shared by many people, for shelter under threatening circumstances. Need was one of the main factors in the integrity of the old, the genuine cabins.

This book does not hope to re-create the mystique, the beauty, the poignancy of log cabins and the life of the people who lived in log cabins, with log outbuildings and the forest all around. All that cannot be brought back. This book can only blaze a trail, dim though it may be, that will possibly lead to a wider appreciation of the housing of the old days and the importance of log cabins in the building of America.

CHAPTER TWO

Cabin Floor Plans

Nineteenth-century steel engraving of a log cabin with a smoke hole instead of a chimney. *Courtesy the New York Public Library*

In the early days of America most of the log cabins built were probably the so-called "turtleback" variety. Or, as Jim Whitley described them in the dialect of his area, "turtle back shacks." Jim knew about this kind of cabin from family legend. Such a cabin had been thrown together by the old man who eventually sold Whitley's grandfather forty acres of land to establish the family homestead. A turtleback shack was den-like in shape, with a low roof and low walls. Probably the logs were unhewn, the corners uneven, the floors of dirt, and the roof made of bark or clumsy shakes rather than riven shingles. Many had only small chimneys built of fieldstone up to a point, with clay-lined logs joining the flue, or perhaps of "cats," bundles of straw soaked in mud and laid like logs to form the chimney. The inside arrangment of such a simple place could hardly be called a plan. It was more a tiny bit of earth isolated from a hostile environment by four rough walls of logs.

But the log cabins of American legend did have definite, if unsophisticated, floor plans, harking back to the traditional peasant houses of medieval England, Scotland, and Ireland. In the Southeast, where log cabins were built over a longer period of time and lived in for more generations than was the case in probably any other region, one could often determine the European origins of a family by the dimensions and the floor plan of its cabin.

Most of the pioneers who settled the vast, variegated woodlands of Georgia, Tennessee, Alabama, the Carolinas, and Virginia were of two main stocks: English and Scotch-Irish. The Scotch-Irish had originally been lowland Scots who, in great numbers, emigrated to Northern Ireland in the sixteenth and seventeenth centuries when England more or less claimed dominance over that still disturbed isle of green fields and proud, bloody violence.

The English had quite a simple floor plan: a square, roughly sixteen feet, with one door, and perhaps, or perhaps not, a window or two, a low

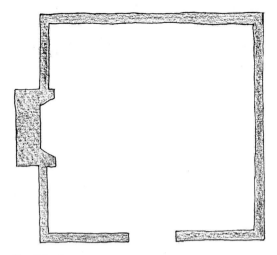

English plan.

ceiling, and a loft, reached by a tiny stairway or more often by a ladder of pegs or boards. Of course, it had the quintessential fireplace, for heat in the wintertime and for cooking in all seasons, in one of the sidewalls. Very often there would be a root cellar beneath the floor, a cave-place for keeping meat, milk, and excess vegetables relatively cool on even the hottest summer days and for protecting potatoes, apples, and pumpkins from frost during the seasons of frost.

The Scotch-Irish, on the other hand, tended to build their cabins to a traditional plan that reflected the higher latitudes and harsher winters of their Scottish ancestors. Most Scotch-Irish cabins were rectangular in shape, usually about sixteen feet by twenty feet. The really distinguishing feature of the Scotch-Irish cabin, however, was the fact that it had two doors, one in front and one directly opposed to it in back. It is said, based on study of medieval Scottish homes, that two doors were favored so that the cows could be brought in for milking in bad weather, presumably being led in the front door and out the back, almost as though the willing beasts were invited in the front door as honored guests when they had bounty to give, and cast out the back door in disgrace when the bounty had been taken.

Of course, the rectangular, two-door cabins, usually with a window or two, had generous hearths of fieldstone, often mortared with clay, in one of the end walls.

The cabin builders of our early days, however, were hardly architectural purists when it came to floor plans. When a man of English derivation married a woman of Scotch-Irish blood, he might very well build her a cabin of rectangular plan when they moved into the wilderness. Also, none of our forebears felt tied to exactly the same type of houses their forebears had occupied in Britain. If more space was needed, a second cabin might be built adjacent to the back door of a Scotch-Irish type dwelling, or a second house might be abutted against the wall of a square cabin, with doors cut to connect the two, although many old houses that started as single-room log cabins had no connecting doors between the rooms, only a well-worn path from one to the other outside the house.

The settlers of English descent, though, seemed to show a little more imagination in using logs for comfortable houses, using a variety of floor

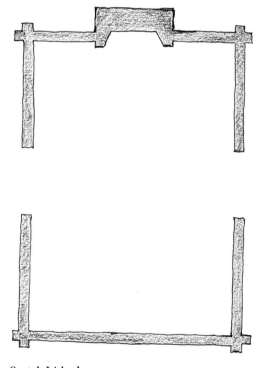

Scotch-Irish plan.

Saddlebag plan.

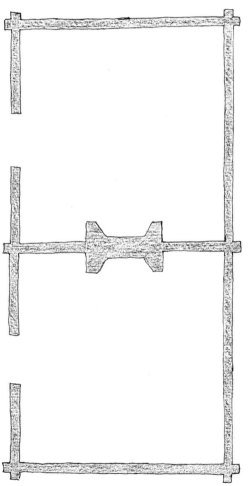

plans that offered more room and more comfort for a family and reflected the old English manor houses in general style.

For instance, one form of cabin on the frontier, mostly the southern frontier, was called a saddlebag house. It consisted of two rooms, or pens, if you will, with a central chimney that provided a hearth for each of the rooms.

Each room had a door and perhaps a window or two and sometimes a connecting door between the rooms located on one side of the chimney. Usually the two rooms shared a common loft, which provided a place for the boys to sleep next to the warm chimney and offered storage space. Sometimes, but seldom, there was a back door to one or both of the rooms.

A variation of the saddlebag style was dubbed the double-pen house. This type also had two separate rooms, its distinction from the saddlebag being that one or both had a hearth located in an end wall. The dividing wall between the two rooms might be of logs or boards, it mattered not, and maybe there was a connecting door between them and maybe not. After all, the proper making of doors required several tools beyond those needed to make a cabin and also required hinges and nails, both in short supply on the early frontier. Windows, as usual, were optional, for a door open summer and winter provided as much light as a window with its expensive glass, and the door did not require washing.

Another design for a log house, which also followed traditional English patterns of house building, was the dogtrot cabin, its colloquial-sounding name belying its potential for elegance. Like the double-pen house it consisted of two rooms, but the rooms were separated, not by a wall but by an open hallway, or dogtrot. Rooms and hallway shared a common floor and were covered by a common roof. Each room generally had a fireplace in its end wall and each had a door opening on the dogtrot.

One can easily imagine how such a floor plan could be altered to fit a large and busy family. Each room, for instance, could be divided into two with two doors to the open hallway and with corner fireplaces in each, using a common flue. The dogtrot could be covered at each end, making it into an interior hall. Then if the walls were raised higher, one could have a two-story, eight-room house of exactly the same basic plan as Washington's beloved and beautiful Mount Vernon.

Double-pen plan.

There were other plans for two-story houses of logs, for not all of them had the central hall, or dogtrot. Sometimes a Scotch-Irish-type cabin would be built high enough to include another story or half-story above the main room, with a fireplace in each of the rooms or only in the lower room, for cold weather did not seem to bother our hearty backwoods ancestors too much and fireplaces were mainly for cooking.

The point is that there was great versatility in the methods of building log cabins and houses, and the pattern could easily be altered to meet the needs of larger families and higher social status.

Part of the evolution of housing in the rural South is reflected in the development of the typical southern "I" house, or plain plantation style, so frequently seen from Virginia through Texas, each of pretty much the same pattern as log houses that would have been built in an earlier generation.

Many of the "I" houses had a **T**- or **L**-shaped floor plan, but this too is derived from plans of log cabins and houses that never felt the touch of an

Dogtrot plan.

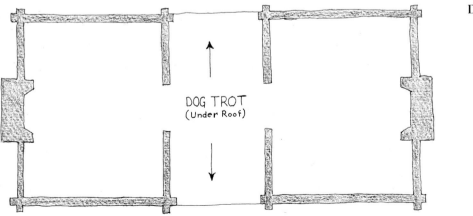

DOG TROT
(Under Roof)

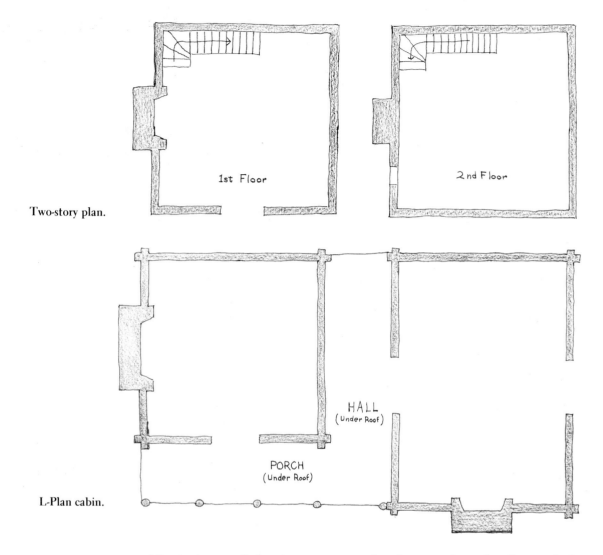

Two-story plan.

1st Floor

2nd Floor

L-Plan cabin.

HALL
(Under Roof)

PORCH
(Under Roof)

architect. A man living in a two-story log house, whose family needed more space, might build an additional cabin behind it. Eventually this would be connected to the initial building by a covered, floored walkway, and later the walkway might be closed, making it into a hall and providing integrity to the whole complex of buildings.

Regardless of the complexity of a log building, most continued to retain root cellars to provide refrigeration, even though separate spring-houses might be built eventually for the same purpose.

As pumpkins might sometimes be changed into coaches, log houses were sometimes changed into mansions by the magic of cosmetic covering. There are many examples of such transformation in the Southeast and probably beyond that region.

After all, why should the solid, insulating construction of a log building be lost when an owner had reached a point of affluence that allowed him to afford a more aristocratic-appearing dwelling place? The conversion was quite simple.

Logs can be hewn with broadax or hatchet or adz before or after they are fitted together to make a building. The owner of a log house, then, could easily dress the outside and inside of his place to allow studs to be nailed to the solid outside wall to which, in turn, clapboards could be nailed, and inside studs could be installed to support laths, which would receive plaster. New windows could easily be cut and framed as could doorways. The open ends of halls and porches could be enclosed, weatherboarded, and plastered to provide more inside space than the old house had offered. With a few alterations, then, the old family house of logs might become almost palatial in its plan and appearance, inside and out, the only clues to its lowly origin being certain hand-hewn joists in floor or ceiling that were forever hidden until the time was reached when plumbing and wiring would be installed.

It is not unheard of in older, settled communities, for workmen preparing to demolish or move an old house to find that underneath the clapboards there are the massive, horizontal logs of an original and long-forgotten cabin.

CHAPTER THREE

Log Outbuildings and Fences

Nineteenth-century steel engraving of a log cabin. *Courtesy the New York Public Library*

Virtually all of the original log cabins that were built were farmhouses that could hardly exist alone. The cabins and more sophisticated edifices were built to shelter humans, but additional buildings for livestock and fowl and working space had to be constructed to make a farm complete. These buildings, barns and corncribs, chicken houses and hog houses, workshops and springhouses, were for the most part made of logs the same as homes were and roofed, albeit not as tightly, with shingles or shakes. The forms of these outbuildings were as varied and as subject to evolution as the cabins, and many, like the cabins, reflected a particular national heritage.

The barns were all of a basic shape with square corners, but they varied widely in size and plan. The simpliest was a single-crib barn with a wide door and perhaps one or two stalls built within. When a wagon was acquired it was often given shelter under an added lean-to roof, supported by one wall of the barn and stout oaken posts set in the mother earth. Sometimes a second lean-to would be built on the opposite side to shelter a small smithy or the lathe and workbench of a woodworking shop.

If a farmer had a couple of horses, a yoke of oxen, and a milk cow or two, along with rock sledges and a wagon, he might build a double-crib barn, two structures perhaps ten feet apart, with dirt floors, sharing a single roof. Stalls could be built in each of the cribs, facing the open space between them, and the open space could be used to store wagons, sledges, plows, whatever. The common loft, floored with boards or puncheons, could be used for storing hay. And, as with the simpler single-crib barn, the larger version could easily be enlarged further by the addition of lean-to sheds on either side.

Large frontier farms located in broad, fruitful valleys, might need four-crib barns, which provided a cross-shaped passageway for easy access, many stalls, and perhaps an interior shop. The whole would be unified with a tremendous, spreading roof that furnished additional outside shelter for firewood or extra shingles, lumber, or equipment. Closing off one of the passageways at both ends converted a four-crib barn into a transverse-crib barn, with less inside storage space but more stalls.

Hog houses were usually rather small, set inside a hog pen of split logs and designed to provide hog families security from wolves, panthers, and bears. The hogs were driven into the house only at night.

Chicken houses were even smaller than hog houses, equipped with pole roosts, egg and hatching nests, and a feed trough. The houses for chickens and turkeys, however, had to be rather tightly built to discourage dogs, weasels, and skunks. They were used for nighttime habitation only, except in the case of laying hens.

Workshops, when detached from other buildings, were usually made of logs hewn not so smoothly as those in a house, and seldom chinked. Usually the workshops had large double doors to permit bringing a wagon inside. Most also had dirt floors.

Logs provided shelter for everyone and everything in the backwoods: people, animals, and equipment. There was never a dearth of building material, and with it each man was his own architect, with a thousand-year tradition of housing to guide him.

Fences

Fences, too, must be considered part of the shelter a home provided in the early days. They did not provide shelter against rain and snow, wind and sun, but against other "elements of nature" such as predatory animals which could slaughter pigs and fowl or easily ruin a promising crop.

With so many logs to spare (they were a nuisance in clearing new fields) and an abundance of land, many farmers of the frontier split logs of many varieties of trees, preferably white oak, walnut, cedar, or locust, to make a worm, or snake, fence around a pasture or cornfield. Worm fences consisted of legions of split rails stacked in a zigzag pattern to a height of four or five feet. The pattern furnished a broad base of four or five feet overall, and the weight of the wood gave substance to the enclosure, or outclosure if one prefers. Since the rails were stacked alternately at the corners, like the corners of a log structure, the openings between the rails

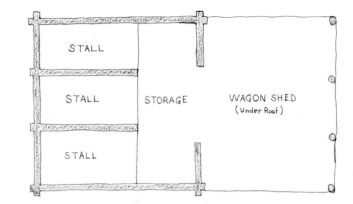

Single-crib barn plan.

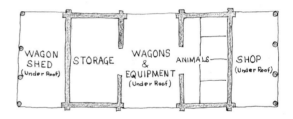

Two-crib barn plan.

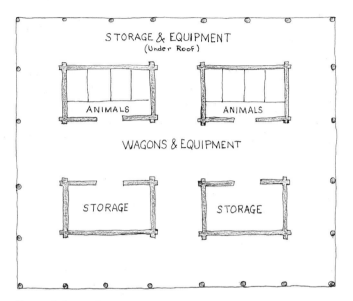

Four-crib barn plan.

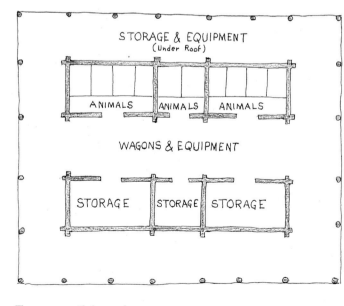

Transverse-crib barn plan.

were small enough to keep free-ranging hogs and cattle out of a field of ripening corn or grain. Since the corners formed by the zigzag could not be plowed, they were relinquished to weeds and small bushes that gave shelter to quail, rabbits, and other small animals that supplemented a frontier diet. Worm fences could easily be torn down and reassembled as fields were expanded or divided.

A more permanent fence was the post and rail, a type that required fewer logs but considerably more work to erect. The name is most descriptive, for such fences were made of posts sunk in the ground eight or ten feet apart, with two or three mortises bored and chiseled into each post to receive the rails. In areas where black locust grew plentifully this wood was invariably used for posts, for it would resist rot and termites in the ground for a hundred years in most cases. Cedar was about as good and was used extensively in the lands of Tennessee and other areas of the Southeast. Post oak, white oak, and chestnut oak, as well as chestnut, would last for from thirty to forty years or more if cut in the dead of winter and were widely used when cedar and locust were unavailable. And although a dedicated woodworker might recoil at the thought, in Ohio and Indiana, where there were virtual leagues of walnut forests, this fine, now-rare furniture tree would be used for fences, for its durability matched that of the oaks. Pine is generally not good material for fence posts or rails, yet in the pine-forested coastal plains of the South heart pine might be used, for the heartwood of a virgin pine is so saturated with rosin that it will last almost forever against anything but fire.

It's obvious, of course, that post and rail fences and even the more closely built snake fences presented no obstacle to rabbits in the vegetable garden or weasels and other small "varmints" that sought access to a chicken dinner. To protect these vital assets the log cabin owner of early years, and of relatively late years in the southern mountains, would construct a pole fence. This stout, almost solid, fencing was comprised of numerous poles two to three inches thick at the butt and six to eight feet long. Each pole was leaned at about a 45-degree angle along the axis of the fence, and each was supported by a "horse" of two crossed sticks that rested on the pole previously installed. Most pole fences were circular, not being suitable for corners, and when the circle or oval was completed, the beginning and end would overlap to form an opening for a gate. Pole fences were always started at one of the gateposts to provide a starting place, since horses and leaning poles had to have support from the start.

Pole fences offered substantial protection against little creatures of the woods and yard and could be moved and repaired with relative ease so long as the nearby woods supplied poles. But when poles were no longer easily available the cabin holder would go back to logs in a different form to build himself a paling fence if he could make or afford the necessary nails.

Most frontier and mountain paling fences were built of roughly hewn or split posts and rails with split palings. The posts were always of rot-resistant wood like locust, post oak, white oak, chestnut, oak, or other woods that split easily. Palings, too, were usually split because of the absence or the cost of a sawmill, and because split palings were more than adequate for the purpose. Besides, the texture of splitting adds a dimension to wood not found in sawn boards.

Fences of split palings could easily be made with the simple tools of cabin building: the ax and froe, glut and maul. Many a log cabin had the appearance of its front yard or back garden enhanced by the sentinel pickets of a paling fence.

The continuing lines of frontier fences served also to give order to the appearance of a farm with its scattered buildings, great and small. The fences, like the buildings, followed the natural landscape, here placed straight across level or slightly rolling fields, there curving to follow a creek bank or to avoid an exposed patch of rock. Fences gave an interesting pattern to a farm and provided integrity to the whole. They were a vital and beautiful feature of log cabin living until gradually barbed wire, hog wire, and chicken wire, mass-produced to sell cheaply but dull and ugly, replaced the old wooden fences a few years before the turn of the twentieth century.

CHAPTER FOUR

Cabin Construction

A well-made log cabin is like a huge, fine blanket chest, its sides smoothed in and out, its corners neatly dovetailed, its lines plumb and square. And, like fine chests, the wood with which cabins are constructed is usually left free of paint, the natural colors gradually changing over the years. Cabins age as gracefully as beautiful people.

The simplest cabins, those thrown up hastily by hunters or the type first built by the Indians, were not like fine chests but more like packing crates. They had no foundation to speak of, no carefully squared corners, no floors other than the forest floor on which they stood. But the majority of log cabins and houses, those that served as home places, were constructed carefully from the ground up, which is one reason many of them lasted for so long.

Building Tools

The more finished a cabin was, the more tools required to build it, but nothing like the variety of tools needed to build a fine house of boards or bricks. Indeed, a rough cabin of logs can be built entirely with a felling ax (preferably of the American pattern with its superior balance), and even rough boards or shakes for the roof can be built from oak or pine or cedar with an ax. But such a cabin would have an unfinished look, its corners ragged, the logs of one wall chopped roughly open to accept a crude, mud-mortared hearth, the doorway crooked and awkward.

Building a cabin that was tight and snug with an appearance that would be a source of pride to a family and display the enviable craftsmanship of the builder required a number of tools that were simple and ingenious in principle but difficult to use properly without years of experience. The quality of workmanship on a cabin reflected the skill of the workman far more than the sophistication of his tools.

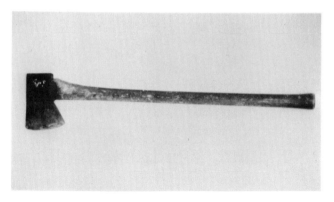

The typical American felling ax, developed in the early colonies as a more efficient tool than the ancient felling ax of Europe.

Right: Crosscut saw used to fell and buck logs and to trim corners on log cabins.

Middle: Broadax with a short handle and an extremely wide blade, used for hewing logs that had been scored by a felling ax.

A felling ax, of course, was the basic tool, for it was essential for felling the trees that formed walls, sills, and joists. In times past trees were cut exclusively with the felling ax and bucked or cut into lengths with the same simple tool. It was easier thus only because of the astounding facility and accuracy with which early Americans used the carefully sharpened American ax. A good axman could wield his tool tirelessly, it seemed, cutting through a huge log in less time than it took two men to divide it with a crosscut saw.

In later times, at the heyday of cabin building on the frontier, the crosscut saw was used more frequently for felling and bucking in conjunction with the indispensable ax. Saws, too, in one form or another, were needed to trim the protrusion of logs at the corners, giving corners a neatness that sometimes would equal that of homes built by highly skilled housewrights in town. Other saws such as bow saws and panel saws and frame saws were needed to precisely cut door and window frames, the boards of shutters and mantles and doors and other construction that required precision. A few pioneers might even have owned and used pit saws to supply rough boards from rough logs. Pit saws were not common on the frontier, but common enough so that they were used in the Virginia mountains even after the turn of the twentieth century.

Most of the partitioned wood in a log cabin, however, was parted by splitting rather than by sawing. Splitting logs for walls and puncheon floors was accomplished by two simple homemade tools, the glut and the maul. Gluts were merely wedges hewn in the woods from three- to four-inch saplings of dogwood, elm, hornbeam, or beech, and on occasion from hickory or oak, though the latter two woods tended to split under repeated mauling. The maul was a club carved from a six-inch tree. Its head, merely a section of the original tree at the root end, was about eight inches long. The handle was shaped by ax and knife from the remainder. With glut and maul one could split the mightiest pine or chestnut, poplar or oak once a starting split to receive the glut had been made by the ax that felled the tree.

Another tool for the more delicate splitting of shingles and shakes was the froe, a bar of iron doubled to form an eye and forge-welded with one of its edges bluntly chamfered. A rough handle was inserted in the eye. The blade was driven into a billet of oak or other shingle-wood with a

Maul and glut, or wooden wedge, used for splitting logs.

small one-handed maul, the billet being held in an acute tree fork known as a brake.

Possibly the most picturesque tool used in cabin building was the broadax, an ancient and effective hewing device that over the centuries had evolved into several different forms, each adhering to the same principle. Several of these forms were used in America, representing the various European cultures that settled the wilderness of the New World. The typical British form, which was like a regular ax with a very broad cutting edge from eight to fifteen inches in length, was the most widely used. But German, French, Swiss, and Swedish settlers often used a goosewing ax in all of its several manifestations. Goosewing axes shared the same broad blade, but the blade was shaped almost like a separate knifelike appendage to the head and on some the blade soared upward from the eye, looking like the spread wing of a goose. Some had eyes like a felling ax, and others had the hickory handle fitted into a deep socket. Most early broadaxes had a chisel, or basil, edge sharpened on only one side, leaving the other side to cut a flat surface on the log being hewn. All these had the short handle curved away from the flat side of the blade to keep fingers from being crushed against the log when the heavy head, weighing up to fifteen pounds, was brought down to do its work. Broadaxes were kept razor-sharp, for otherwise the tool could not function with maximum efficiency.

Another tool often, but not always, used in constructing a log cabin was the foot adz, a tool with origins in the Stone Age. This, too, was a hewing tool, but for more refined work than that of the broadax. Indeed, an expert adzman could turn out joists and floorboards with a surface comparable to a board finished with a plane. The adz resembled a hoe or

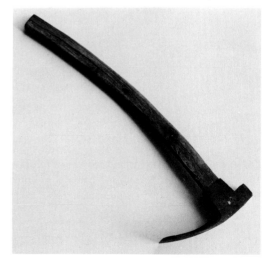

Above: A froe such as this was used for riving small boards as well as the shingles and shakes for roofing a cabin. Froes were easily made at a home blacksmith shop or by a general blacksmith.

Below: For finer hewing the foot adz was employed instead of the broadax. Foot adzes were used particularly for smoothing floorboards in cabins. The curved handle was a common feature of this tool, although many homemade handles were straight.

mattock in form, but was actually a chisel equipped with a handle so that the carefully sharpened edge could be swung to slice away the inequalities on top of a timber.

Usually a cabin builder would also own an auger or two, with spoon bits before the American Revolution and Scottish twist bits after 1800. Nails were so scarce in the days when they were handmade that pegs, or trunnels, were used instead for installing door and window frames. The auger, of course, bored the holes that received the trunnels, and it bored holes in the solid walls for pegs on which clothes were hung.

In roofing, when the split shingles were nailed to the purlins, a carpenter's hammer, a tool with possibly the oldest pedigree of any of man's tools, was most necessary.

Woods Used

Tall, straight trees were needed for building, and though many different species were considered suitable, the most frequently used were oak, pine, cedar, chestnut, and yellow poplar. On occasion, however, log houses in certain parts of Ohio and Indiana were built entirely of black walnut logs, a building material that would make any house distinctive.

The durability of a log cabin depended on its sills, the two logs that rested on the foundation wall or piers to support the walls. Sills were of white or chestnut oak, cedar, walnut, chestnut, or locust, for these woods defied rot for many, many years. Usually sill logs were a bit larger than the wall logs, again to ensure the long life of the entire structure, for the sills could not be easily replaced if they began to deteriorate.

Most cabins had walls of pine logs. Scattered pine trees were plentiful in the hardwood forests of the Piedmont and uplands east of the Great Plains, and tall, straight pines predominated in the coastal plains of the South. The hill and mountain country yielded what the early pioneers called forest pine, an ideal timber for cabin building. Actually it was a loblolly or Virginia pine in most instances, but when growing among hardwoods it was forced to shoot up straight and tall to find the sunlight so essential to pine growth. The trunks rose for thirty or forty feet before a branch appeared, and many in the virgin forests of the New World would

Augers bored holes for many purposes around a log cabin: for installing clothes pegs, for fastening floorboards, for starting mortises. This one is a Scotch bit auger, a type invented about 1819.

The sort of hammer that would have been found around frontier cabins before the adz-eye hammer was invented ca. 1840.

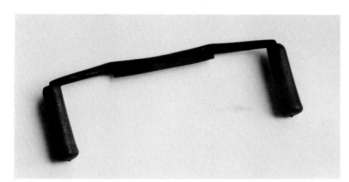

A drawing knife that was used to smooth poles and slats and sometimes shingles.

be two to three feet in diameter at the butt. Such giants developed a smoother bark than young trees; this development may have led to the misconception that they were a separate variety of pine.

In the southern Appalachians many cabins and other buildings were built entirely of chestnut logs, including sills, for the chestnut grew straight and large, sometimes reaching six feet in diameter at the butt. Also, it seemed to last forever.

Cedar, which grew thickly in the limestone region of Tennessee and in other scattered areas, was used widely for small cabins, for it was easily hewn and as defiant of rot as white oak and chestnut. An added advantage was the delightful aromatic odor of the hewn logs, which discouraged insects of all sorts.

Possibly the most beautiful cabins of all had walls of yellow poplar, or tulip poplar as it is often called. This tree grows widely in the woods of the Southeast and Middle Atlantic states. Poplar rots quickly when damp, so cabins made of it always had sills of some durable wood, but as wall logs seasoned poplar lasts for centuries.

Other types of trees, such as oak and birch, were rarely used in cabin building, although cottonwood was frequently used in the West.

Laying the Foundation

There was a method to preparing the materials and assembling a log house. First of all the foundation was built of stones, either of dry wall construction or mortared with clay. Usually the foundation walls were a foot or more in thickness, many of them with a door opening that gave access to a root cellar dug four or five feet into the ground before the cabin was raised and later lined with shelves for the storage of food and drink. Foundations might be raised two feet from the ground level, but the bottom stones rested on solid subsoil six or eight inches below the level of the ground.

In areas where stone was scarce the cabin might be set on piers of rock that rested on subsoil and rose a foot or two above the earth, leaving a fine space beneath the floor for dogs and chickens, or perhaps young pigs to find shelter from the elements, or providing a place to store tools and washtubs and other essentials for civilized living. And when stone was simply nonexistent, piers of white oak or chestnut oak or even rosin-impregnated heart pine might be used.

Foundations and piers were carefully checked for level as they were built, using a plumb level or perhaps just a pan of water, although the sills were also leveled carefully when they were put in place.

Hewing the Logs

When the selected trees were cut, a little longer than actually needed, they were usually, but not always, hauled by oxen or horses to the cabin site for hewing. Sometimes they might be hewn where they were felled, but it was easier to keep the hewing tools in one place, and the chips were excellent for kindling fires.

There must have been a certain aesthetic pleasure to hewing logs for a cabin, with a profound satisfaction to be gained from transforming the huge, natural logs to manageable dimensions with only a felling ax and a broadax. The type of tree would add to or detract from the pleasure.

For instance, hewing oak for sills, even while green and relatively amenable to the ax, takes longer than shaping some of the softer woods. Dimensions are first marked with a chalk line, the snapping of the taut string marking the rough bark so that scoring and later hewing can be controlled. Scoring consists of sinking the bit of the felling ax a couple of inches in the side of the round log, the axman swinging from above, letting the momentum and weight of his tool do the work for him. Then the broadax is employed, working from the side, to slice out the wood between the scoring cuts. On large logs each side might have to be scored and hewn several times to remove the excess wood on the outside of the chalk mark.

Oak is a tough but grainy wood. The felling ax does not sink so readily through its grain as with other trees and the razor-sharp broadax does not slice quite so easily. Yet good timbers can be hewn from oak, the surface smooth except for the vertical blemishes from the scoring, the grain showing its wavy pattern, the resulting plane smooth and straight.

Chestnut has many of the characteristics of oak in hewing, though it might be considered a bit softer and easier to work.

Forest pine is different. It, too, has a prominent grain, but the wood is much softer and easier to score and hew. Probably a pine log can be hewn in half the time it takes to shape oak of the same size, one of the reasons that pine was so often used for wall logs in a cabin. Also, large pines grow taller than oaks and have longer trunks free from limbs in most cases. When large enough, a pine can be split into two logs, the two resulting timbers always being placed on opposite sides at the same level when the cabin is raised, the flat split side hewn as well as the round sides.

Cedar also is soft enough to be easily hewn, but cedar logs are hardly ever large enough to split.

The most satisfying wood to work is yellow poplar. Poplar tends to grow in patches interspersed with other hardwoods, so if a patch grew near a cabin site it was simple to pick and fell enough of the towering trunks at one spot to make a cabin. Almost invariably poplar trees grow arrow-straight with perhaps thirty feet on mature specimens before a limb is found. And they grow big in diameter, sometimes to four feet at the butt. The wood splits readily though not quite so easily as pine, oak, or cedar.

But hewing poplar is where the broadaxman finds infinite satisfaction. When green, the wood cuts like butter and with its light yellow color and creamy texture even looks a little like butter fresh from the churn. The odor of green poplar is somewhat stringent, a clean smell that offers yet another pleasure to its working.

More often than not poplar was hewn into heavy boards, perhaps four to six inches in thickness and anywhere from thirty to thirty-six inches in width. With two such boards from each trunk, just three or four trees could easily yield enough material for a comfortable cabin. Backwoods housewives must have particularly liked poplar cabins, because the hewn wood of the interior surfaces of the logs was light-colored and clean and remained lighter than most woods when time had colored it a soft gray.

Raising the Cabin

One man and his family could usually fell the trees, hew the logs, build the foundation wall and dig the cellar, granted enough time. Raising a cabin, however, required strength, part of it provided by horses and oxen but most of it furnished by men, the men of neighboring farms. Because the opportunity for gatherings was so infrequent in the backwoods, and because attending gatherings required so much travel and preparation, a cabin raising was usually treated as a rare social event. The same festive spirit was accorded barn raisings, also, or the assembly of any other large buildings. Indeed, long after the frontier had passed and barns were built of sawn lumber and nailed together, barn raisings continued to be a tradition and a major social event for the families of a rural community.

With twenty or thirty men and several teams of oxen a cabin could be raised and roofed in a day, finished except for possibly the hearth and chimney, which were usually built last. And while the men and older boys worked on the cabin, the women cooked a huge meal over an open fire, and young children stood by to fetch tools and small materials. There was almost always some malingering on the part of young men and young women who were expected to take advantage of the occasion to do a little courting. Otherwise a young man might have to walk or ride for miles to call on the lady of his choice.

The first thing, of course, in raising a building was to lay the massive sill logs upon foundation or piers. Once in place the sills were carefully leveled and distance between front and back sills precisely measured to ensure that they were parallel, for if the sills were not positioned with care the whole cabin might end up askew. Sill logs were mortised for floor joists and the joists installed before the walls went up. Flooring would be laid as almost the last operation.

Once the sills were properly laid the rest of the logs could be put up with relative facility. The first two end logs, of course after being notched flat on the bottom to fit the sills, also had to be checked to see that they were parallel, and of course they had to be of the same size, but choosing them was no great problem, for the cabin owner had already matched his logs pretty well when he had hewn them, matching them two by two and perhaps numbering each to see that they shared the same course in opposite walls.

Notching

Notching served two purposes. First of all it allowed the logs to be locked together at the corners to provide immutable solidity. Also, it

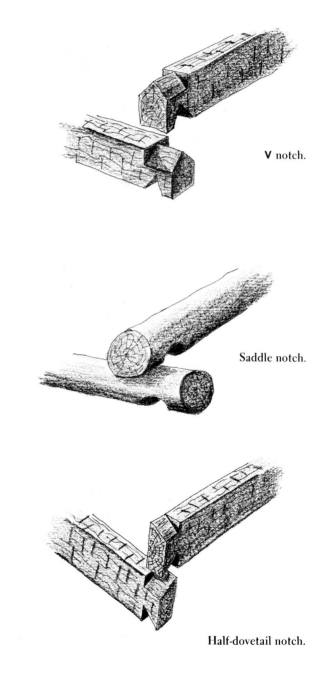

V notch.

Saddle notch.

Half-dovetail notch.

Full-dovetail notch.

Flat or square notch.

French Canadian post and log construction.

minimized the interstices between the logs and saved on the amount of chinking needed. And, as with floor plans, the three main types of notching reflected to some extent the cultural background of the cabin builder.

Simple saddle notches are found widely in areas of northeast Georgia, for instance, areas that were settled by the intrepid Scotch-Irish, who moved in mostly from North and South Carolina in the late 1830s to take over Cherokee lands. Northwest Georgia, on the other hand, was settled mainly by families of English descent, and the cabins of that area are fitted together mostly by half-dovetail notching. The meticulous German settlers at Old Salem, North Carolina, and those in Virginia and Pennsylvania often used a full-dovetail. Of the three, the half-dovetail was considered best because the outward slope of the notches allowed rainwater to drain away before it could cause rotting. Often, however, a cabin might be notched with half-dovetails while the corncrib, barn, and hog house might have saddle notching, which was easier to do.

Besides the three types of notching described, one sometimes found a cabin with square or flat notches. This was the easiest type to make by far since it could be done by making a straight saw cut and splitting out the small portion the cut delineated. But square notches did not lock the logs together and could not be considered a sound construction method for a regular cabin.

And indeed, cabins with square corner notchings were not intended for log cabins or houses in the true sense when they were originally raised.

A study of square-notched cabins reveals a number of common characteristics that fit a particular function for the structures. For instance, virtually all are constructed of logs finely hewn to a square section of from six to eight inches. When notched and joined, this size timber leaves interstices between the logs of about two inches, much wider and more even than the interstices of typical frontier log buildings. The corners of square-notched buildings are precisely plumb and the wall surfaces, inside and out, are invariably far more even than on backwoods structures. Many square-notched log houses have had channels hewn vertically in certain wall logs, obviously for the attachment of furring strips to which clapboards could be nailed.

The conclusion to be drawn from a careful observation of square-notched log houses is inescapable and incontrovertible but largely unrecorded. Such structures were intended from the beginning to be house frames, as a substitute for the massive mortised, tenoned, and pegged frames that provided the skeleton for most fine weatherboarded houses built in America prior to 1840.

Most of the square-notched houses seen were built between 1790 and 1820, a period when the American frontier was moving rather rapidly to the West, at a time when the accumulated capital of the tidewater regions could allow some affluent families to invest in new lands in the wilderness and also to build a better house once they had reached the new lands. But there were difficulties in building fine houses in the wilderness, mainly a lack of skilled housewrights with their sophisticated tools and techniques that were found in the established eastern communities. Where, in the wilderness, would one find the skilled carpenters with proper tools to form and join accurately the precise framing needed to support an enduring house?

One could not find them, but on the other hand the frontier could yield plenty of men equipped with and skilled in the use of felling ax, broadax, and froe—men capable of building a very neat pen of logs. So the log pen was built by local labor and covered with weatherboarding to create a house as strong and as handsome as any in the East. The square notches made neater corners, which were locked when the weatherboarding was nailed to the frame. The wide, even interstices between the hewn timbers provided space for nogging, a combination of brick and mortar that was often used to fill the mortised frames of eastern houses and that provided added strength and insulation. And one could live comfortably within such a frame for a year or two if the installation of weatherboarding was delayed.

This conclusion may be supported by several of the log houses pictured in Part Two of this book, notably the library at Lumpkin, Georgia, the Isaac Hill House at Calloway Gardens, the Durst House in Atlanta, and the magnificent John Ross House at Rossville, Georgia.

Hewn log frames for fine houses offer an elegance not found in the cabin of the pioneer, perhaps, but they fit neatly and interestingly into the log cabin culture of America.

Notching was usually done on the ground following careful measurements as each log was raised and put into position. Usually, though, some fitting was necessary when the log was raised, a little shaving here and there with the ax. In some cabins the corners were so well fitted that they seemed to have been joined in a cabinetmaker's shop.

Ax and saw and, at times, an adz were used for notching, with the ax often being employed alone. One wonders how only an ax can be used to cut accurate notches, with the angles of the dovetails fitting snugly even though the adjoining logs are necessarily separated when the notching is done, quite unlike the trying and final fitting of furniture joints on a workbench. The answer is training and skill. Virtually all American frontiersmen and farmers in later days, before chain saws, were practically born with axes in their hands. The ax was the essential tool of the frontier, far more important to living than the symbolic long rifle. It was used to cut firewood almost every day, for either cooking or heating. It was used to clear fields when a man settled new land in the wilderness, and it was used to shape the logs of house and outbuildings. Almost any adult backwoodsman could use an ax with uncanny precision and as a true extension of himself, cutting as deeply as he wanted, at whatever angle he desired, cutting thin shavings or chips the size of dinner plates. A good axman, like any craftsman, paid much attention to the condition of the tool. Axes had to be kept sharp enough to shave with or they would not function properly. Handles were usually carefully made by the axman himself to fit his own physiology, and one man would seldom use another's ax any more than another's shoes because it simply would not fit.

Fitting the Logs in Place

Cabins are started by building an elegant pigpen in effect. The logs of each wall are fitted two by two, with no openings for doors or windows.

Looking at the sometimes massive logs high up in the wall of a cabin, one sometimes wonders how on earth all that weight, even heavier when it was new and green, could ever have been lifted into place without some monstrous crane. Well, those logs were lifted by using the same basic methods that served mankind for ten thousand years: man's own strength used in concert, the strength of his draft animals, and such ancient devices as the inclined plane and the lever.

Most cabins and houses of logs had the heavier timbers on the bottom courses of the walls, including the usual oaken sills, which represented a great deal of weight. These were dragged by horse or oxen to a spot close to the foundation and parallel to the intended wall. Once in that position a timber up to twenty feet long, fifteen inches wide, and eight to ten inches thick could be raised rather easily by ten men and set on the foundation. An important factor in this was that all the men had spent their lives working, and their bodies were strong and their methods sensible. They knew how to lift without strain, and they knew how to lift together. And if ten men were not available, four men could do the job by using levers to lift the log to the height of the new course, where it could be slid off the levers into position.

Such techniques worked well enough to place logs up to shoulder height, but above that other methods were employed. For instance, skids, or inclined planes, made of poles or split logs, could be placed on the top log of an unfinished wall. The next log could then be placed across the skids and either be pushed up by several men with pikes or pulled up by ropes attached to oxen or horses. Often oxen were used to pull while a few men guided the log.

When the end walls reached shoulder height, which did not take too long if enough men and oxen were used, construction was stopped temporarily. Wedges were driven between the logs of one end six or eight feet apart, or if nails were available two boards or split logs were nailed across the logs to hold them in place, and the crosscut saw was fetched. Then the opening for the hearth was cut, for it was neater to have the hearth open in a solid wall than to try to fit short logs together for the walls on each side of the hearth and possibly ruin the perfect plumb of the corners. When the opening was cut, several men fit adzed or perhaps sawn boards to the cut ends of the logs on each side, nailing or pegging these boards to the log ends to provide a frame for the stonework that followed.

The same procedure was used to cut door and window openings as the walls were raised even higher. In early cabins, following the pattern of British farm cottages, doors were often no higher than five feet and seldom higher than six feet. Doors, however, were sawn very carefully so that the pegged or nailed door frames would be plumb. Windows, on the other hand, were usually small, no more than two logs in height, and these could be sawn and framed very quickly. A meticulous builder would mortise his door and window jambs into the top log, which formed the lintel, providing both strength and aesthetic satisfaction.

On one-and-a-half- or two-story cabins, provisions had to be made for the second-story floor joists when the walls had reached a height of about seven feet. In most cases the mortises for the joists were cut before the front and back logs were put in place, and the joists themselves were installed before the next logs were placed. Some second-floor joists were simply round logs, carefully peeled and hewn flat on the top. The ends would be squared to fit into the mortises. The ends of these joists were usually, but not always, visible from the outside of the cabin. And even if a cabin was planned for one story, ceiling joists were needed. These were mortised in exactly the same manner.

The French method of building cabins required a little more time and a few more tools. First four posts, hewn square and channeled with adz or chisel on opposite sides, would be sunk upright in the ground at points that marked the centers of the intended walls, or at the corners. Center poles were used if logs available were small and short, corner posts if long logs grew close by. (Corner posts, of course, had channels chiseled into adjacent surfaces to fit the corners that emanated from them.)

After posts were sunk the wall logs could be put in place, each with its inside end hewn to fit into the channels and with its corner end square-notched or saddle-notched. As ends were fitted into the channel both members were bored with an auger, and pegs, or trunnels, inserted to join logs and post together. When corner-post construction was followed, the wall logs had to be cut more precisely to length. To facilitate joining logs and post it is probable that the logs were canted slightly as course was laid on course so that the hewn ends could be fitted into the channels, and probably the logs were cut to an exact length that would enable them to be put into place without straining the corner posts outward.

Early Swedish cabins demonstrated the use of channeled posts, or a variation thereof, when rooms were added to a traditionally constructed cabin. In this situation two stout posts were sunk at each corner of the original cabin that would face the new room. The new room would be built with its two exterior corners saddle-notched in the usual manner. Corners that abutted the original pen, however, would be formed by slipping hewn ends between the two posts and pegging them into place. The outside post of each corner would also be pegged to the existing pen.

Another interesting affinity between French and Swedish cabins was that most, but not all, of them constructed fireplaces and chimneys entirely within the walls so that no massive stonework could be seen outside as with English and Scotch-Irish cabins. In effect, French and Swedes built permanent stone or brick stoves inside the room rather than a regular hearth, built into an opening in one end wall. The only difference between the two was that Swedish fireplaces were often built in a corner of the pen, whereas the French favored hearths placed in the center of the room close to an end wall.

There was also a similarity between the construction of the ancient type Swedish granary, consisting of two rooms within a pen, and a few log barns built by farmers of English or Scotch-Irish extraction in the Southeast. The Swedish granaries were divided by a log wall that fitted securely into notches cut into the outside wall logs. Occasionally one finds this same method used in later barns, notably the barn at the Tullie Smith House Restoration in Atlanta. The same method of division was used in building rare double-pen houses that had two rooms, each with a fireplace at its outer end. It is impossible to document whether this method of making two rooms with a log wall integrated within the basic structure was a direct inheritance from the Swedes or an independently arrived at concept.

Roofing

Any building, including log cabins, is made of innumerable large and small pieces. Several thousand shingles, for instance, are needed for a roof. If they had not been riven by the cabin owner before the raising, then neighbors who were expert board makers might take on the task while other guests raised logs. A good board maker can turn out up to two thousand shingles a day, especially if a boy is there to split out bolts from sections of the board tree and separate the sapwood and heartwood from the board wood so that the shingle maker had only to apply his froe and maul to each bolt and concentrate on riving shingles.

Shingles can be made from green white oak, red oak, chestnut, pine, or cedar, and occasionally from yellow poplar. However, the oak, chestnut, and cedar were preferred in the old days because they lasted longer. Shingles were nailed in place while green because this lessened the chance of splitting them when a nail was driven through the thin wood.

Once the rafters were in place and the purlins nailed down the roof could be covered with good split shingles in an hour or so by a swarm of men hammering away. If the shingles were of long-lasting wood, a new roof might not be needed for fifty or seventy-five years.

Frontier cabins before the year 1800 seldom had shingles nailed on. For one reason, nails had to be handwrought one at a time at the forge before cut nails were invented in 1790. Indeed, in early Virginia there was a law that required an abandoned house to be burned in order to salvage precious nails. Only after cheap, mass-produced cut nails became widely available were the roofs of backwoods cabins nailed.

Before that time cabin roofs were often covered with boards or shakes, made by froe and maul, like shingles but as much as four feet long and much wider and thicker than shingles. Frequently the earlier cabins had gable ends of logs, instead of boards, notched at the ends to receive heavy log purlins, with perhaps only three purlins to a side. The long shakes were laid on these just like shingles, but instead of being nailed they were held in place by long straight poles that were lashed with bark or rope at each end to the purlins, thus holding the roof on. Such roofs often had only two course of boards, but they were quite rainproof.

There have been a few reported thatched roofs on American cabins, but thatching was a rare occurrence in the New World.

For some reason, possibly a mere change in fashion, the angle of log cabin roofs changed about 1850, at the time gable ends began to be closed with vertical instead of horizontal sawn boards. Original cabins had rather low roofs, the angle of the gable being near sixty degrees. Shortly before the Civil War, however, new cabins began having roofs of nearer a forty-five-degree angle, the rafters being nailed to a ridgepole where, before, they had been joined at the angle with a trunnel without a ridgepole. The exception to this, of course, was in early cabins with log gable ends and log purlins, which did have a center purlin that served as a ridgepole. In this case, however, there were no rafters.

Chinking

While the roof was being put on, the women and girls, as well as the men and boys who had no other jobs at the time, would be busy chinking the interstices between the logs. If the cracks were wide, poles would be jambed into them and then mud or moss would be packed around the poles, making the walls weathertight. Travelers' accounts of journeying through the South in the early years of the nineteenth century reveal that many cabins of the warm coastal plain had no chinking whatever. The advantage was more illumination in a windowless room in the daytime. At night, inside light shining through the cracks made a home place easy to find for late travelers.

Rarely, cabins were built with no chinking but with the cracks sealed by nailing boards or shingles over them on the inside wall. There is a log cabin near Roswell, Georgia, that was once used as a school and that had its cracks sealed by boards running the length of the walls. It is said that during the three-month school term before World War I, in warm weather, these boards would be temporarily removed to provide more light for the scholars.

Hearth and Chimney

The hearth and chimney were usually the last components of a cabin to be constructed, and possibly the most time-consuming. If sufficient rock had been collected by the owner before the raising, the chimney might be built in a couple of days by neighbors who were good stonemasons, being mortared with clay in remote areas or cement if transport and money were available. Along coastal regions, cement, which was much superior to mud, could be made from shells and, in certain regions, from limestone, but clay made a fine mortar if the stones were fitted carefully.

On some occasions the owner might build his own chimney after the cabin had been raised and roofed, his wife cooking outdoors over an open fire until the hearth was finished. If wintry weather made outdoor cooking unsuitable, the owner and his neighbors might make a temporary hearth and chimney of logs lined with clay until the weather allowed him to make an enduring chimney of stone.

After the cabin had been put together, the owner and his sons could take their time making doors and window shutters, placing pegs on the inside walls for hanging clothes, and placing shelves where needed.

A log cabin, like any other house, was never really quite finished. But it could be constructed and made livable and even comfortable in one or two days with adequate man and animal power and a minimum of tools. Once cabins were put together, most of them lasted for generations. They eliminated the possibility of a housing shortage and were the perfect sort of indigenous shelter for the wilderness of the New World.

CHAPTER FIVE

Log Cabin Living

"Emigrants poured in from different parts, cabins were put up in every direction, and women, children, and goods tumbled into them. The tide of emigration flowed like water through a breach in a mill-dam. Every thing was bustle and confusion, and all at work that could work. In the midst of all this, the mumps, and perhaps one or two other diseases, prevailed and gave us a seasoning. Our cabin had been raised, covered, part of the cracks chinked, and part of the floor laid when we moved in, on Christmas day! There had not been a stick cut except in building the cabin. We had intended an inside chimney, for we thought the chimney ought to be in the house. We had a log put across the whole width of the cabin for a mantel, but when the floor was in we found it so low as not to answer, and removed it. Here was a great change for my mother and sister, as well as the rest, but particularly my mother. She was raised in the most delicate manner in and near London, and lived most of her time in affluence, and always comfortable. She was now in the wilderness, surrounded by wild beasts; in a cabin with about half a floor, no door, no ceiling over head, not even a tolerable sign for a fireplace, the light of day and the chilling winds of night passing between every two logs in the building, the cabin so high from the ground that a bear, wolf, panther, or any animal less in size than a cow, could enter without even a squeeze. . . . Our situation . . . was bettered but by very slow degrees."

From "Our Cabin; or, Life in the Woods,"
The American Pioneer, A Monthly Periodical,
October, 1843.

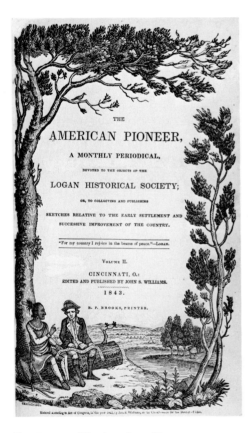

Front cover, *The American Pioneer,*
October 1843. *Courtesy the New York
Public Library*

The population of the United States grew tremendously from 1790, when the country boasted between two and three million people, to 1830, a mere forty years later, when the population reached thirty million. Some of this growth can be attributed to emigration from European nations, but primarily it was due to the phenomenally large families reared by both native and immigrant couples. And many of these millions born on American soil in those forty years were born in log cabins.

There is a small poplar cabin now being restored near Atlanta. It is only fifteen by eighteen feet, and was originally built in Gilmer County, Georgia, in the early ninetenth century. Twenty-one children were reared in this tiny house over two generations. Except perhaps in the most squalid slums in modern cities, it is hard to imagine families of this size being born and reared in such conditions. Yet most of the cabins of the American frontier had no more space than a one-room kitchenette apartment today, with the addition of a loft. We can speculate on why the large families of log cabin dwellers did not turn out bands of criminals, given what modern sociologists have told us about the negative effects of overcrowding. Well, the conditions of frontier life were quite different from the urban environment of the twentieth century. Attitudes were different, too, as were the traditions and social philosophy of cabin dwellers.

Most of the Americans and Europeans who moved to the wilderness

This painting by Wilbur G. Kurtz shows the dogtrot cabin of an early settler near Atlanta and several of the accouterments of log cabin living. The washtub of cast iron and the oak rinsing tub were typical. In most early cabins in the South gourds were hung from tall poles to encourage the nesting of purple martins, a native bird with an instinctive hostility toward crows and hawks. A colony of martins near a cabin protected both the garden and the chicken yard.

and built log cabins came from large families reared in small dwellings. For the most part they were of farming stock. Many of the British, Scotch-Irish, and Welsh, and the Germans, Swiss, and Dutch had parents or grandparents of large families who had been brought up in small, smoky one-room cots in the British Isles and on the continent. These people were used to crowded homes and probably would not have enjoyed the privacy we value so highly in our times. Indeed, in the days before mechanized farming it was an advantage and an ambition to have a large family, for without the extra hands there was no hope for economic prosperity and no hope of security in old age. One appreciated rather than resented one's large family, for each sibling could contribute to the other's well-being. Cabin families were self-sufficient in a way quite different from modern families. And in America things were much better anyway, for though the living quarters might be somewhat crowded the spacious forests were not.

Of course, the more people there were living in one place, the more need for furniture, food, clothes, and bed coverings. Most, and in some cases all, of these items could usually be acquired either from the surrounding woods and fields or from a neighbor in a settlement that might extend over five or ten square miles.

Take the matter of beds, mattresses, and coverings. Any pioneer who could build his own house could also make his own bed. The woods around yielded walnut and beautiful cherry wood, the American mahogany, maple, and easily worked yellow poplar. With an ax, an auger, and one chisel a man could cut a tree, fashion post and rails and headboards, and make himself a rope bed or two. On occasion he could also make his own rope from the inner bark of the hickory.

Beds were very prized possessions in the old days and figured prominently in the estate lists of men and women who died in the eighteenth and early nineteenth centuries. Even in the backwoods a little more care was lavished on making a bed than on making some other articles of furniture. Frequently the head of the family would rig himself a simple pole lathe, ancient in concept and practical in use, and with this produce the bedposts or perhaps a spool bed.

The women in a frontier family made all of the bedcoverings and the mattresses. Every backwoods lady, up until the early years of the

Facing page: Displayed in the Pioneer Museum at the Great Smoky Mountains National Park, this old photograph shows a typical Smoky Mountains homestead of the 1890s.

Many southern log cabins had rather handsome beds such as this one in a corner of the cabin at Stone Mountain Park in Georgia. This bed might have been made at home by a skilled farmer or ordered from a journeyman cabinetmaker who would periodically take a wagonload of wood and tools around an area and make furniture to order for backwoods families. The chair is typical of those on many nineteenth-century farms that were turned at home on a pole lathe, the slats split and mortised into the posts.

Opposite page: Everything shown in this 1890s photograph taken in the Smoky Mountains was made by the father of the family: cabin, shingles, fence.

twentieth century in many areas, sooner or later acquired a spinning wheel and a loom, both an integral part of cabin furnishings, and with them made the material for mattress bags, blankets, quilts, and sometimes sheets, although the quilts usually took the place of sheets. Before a farm was well established the mattresses were filled with hay or corn shucks or, in the bayou country, with Spanish moss. Later most farms kept a flock of geese, which were periodically plucked for down, which made a warmer and more comfortable mattress than noisy corn shucks or straw, and was also used to fill the quilts.

Until the cotton gin was invented toward the end of the eighteenth century flax was grown on most backwoods farms and from it was spun the linen thread with which cloth for bedding and clothes was woven. As soon as possible a backwoods farmer would usually establish a small flock of sheep to provide wool for his wife's and daughters' weaving, and from this was woven the beautifully patterned coverlets that gave color to the room.

After the year 1800 most farms had a patch of cotton, which took the place of linen. The thread, before being woven, was colored with the abundance of dye-producing plants and minerals in America. Every frontier woman knew exactly the shade of yellow she could get from goldenrod, the brown from walnut hulls, and the crimson from pokeberries. Blue generally came from indigo, which was raised on the coastal plantations of the South and which had to be traded for from itinerant peddlers.

Other furniture in the cabin included chairs, usually with ladder backs, blanket chests, stools, benches, and a table, which was used for preparing the food and for dining. Almost all of the furniture was made on the place by father or sons, though some was bought from journeymen cabinetmakers when prosperity permitted.

Chairs were usually made of oak or hickory or a combination of the two woods. The posts were peeled saplings or bolts split out of a larger log and carefully whittled round or turned on the pole lathe, which permitted the turning of a decorative capital on the back posts. According to frontier standards the best chairs had the posts made of green wood that shrank when drying to hold immutably the dry rails and braces. Such a chair would never come apart. This method of assembly without glue was used in the famous Hitchcock chairs that graced more elegant homes than

One of the favorite patterns for the homemade quilts that graced the beds of many settlers' homes from about 1850 on was named "Log Cabin." This pattern had many variations, including "Windmill Blades," "Barn Raising," "Courthouse Steps," "Pineapple," "Sunshine and Shadows," "Straight Furrow," and others. The log cabin quilt at left exhibits a "Light and Dark" variation—the vertical shading is intended to resemble the log walls of a cabin. Its date and origin are unknown.

The log cabin pattern quilt shown here is of the "Barn Raising" variation. Mrs. Fannie Huff made this little-used, all silk bedcover in about 1850. Mrs. Huff's grandniece, Mrs. Eleanor Stout McRae, had the piece rebacked in 1960. It was given to the Atlanta Historical Society by Floyd W. McRae, Jr., in 1977. *Courtesy Atlanta Historical Society, Tullie Smith House Collection*

cabins. The slats in the ladder-back chairs of woodland cabins were split exactly as shingles were and then smoothed and shaped with drawknife or plane or at times with a sharp knife. Seats were made of woven cattails or oak splints or frequently by lacing a green calf or deer hide, which dried and gave additional strength to the whole piece.

Boards for chests and tables were sometimes split from carefully selected wood with straight grain or pit sawn or bought from a nearby water-driven sash saw mill if a community had grown to a point to support a sawmill. Chests were usually dovetailed together and fitted with hinges of wood unless a blacksmith shop was handy to furnish hinges of iron. Tables were mortised or pegged together for the most part, but since tables were more functional than decorative, many tables had the top nailed to the rails, which were mortised into the legs.

Benches and stools made no claim to elegance. Sometimes they were made of boards, but often they consisted of a half log, hewn or adzed

Examples of the utensils used for cooking on the hearth during the log cabin era. Pots, kettles, and Dutch ovens were made of cast iron; shovels, wafer irons, and trivets of wrought iron were forged by the blacksmith.

smooth on the split side and fitted with stout legs driven into auger holes.

Closets were nonexistent in log cabins and clothes presses quite rare. The family's clothes were usually hung on pegs driven into auger holes in the logs of the walls, one wall perhaps being for the women's scant wardrobes, another wall for the men's.

Since self-reliance was the key to survival in frontier times, a cabin owner usually created some sort of shop as soon as his cabin was finished. Sometimes this would be a mere bench set up outside under a large tree, with two posts nearby to form a lathe, a springy branch of the tree used to spin the work. Many early farmers had a respectable knowledge of blacksmithing and would build an outside forge of wood and stone, having the bellows easily removable for storage under the eaves of the cabin when not in use. Then, as soon as time permitted, he would build a respectable shop in a lean-to on the barn or of logs, just as his cabin had been built. But the outdoors was as much a part of cabin living as the cabin itself, and most cabin dwellers retained outdoor workbenches and worked there whenever weather permitted, regardless of the existence of a shop building.

A majority of backwoodsmen, including the Appalachian farmers of the early twentieth century, seemed to be natural craftsmen, perhaps out of necessity. They were always making something because so much was needed to be comfortable on an isolated farm, and there were few stores and little money to spend in the stores that were. Aside from that, many of these farmers liked to make things.

They made the shoes for their families; they made dough bowls and rolling pins; they made farm equipment and tools for the shop. And when there was enough leisure they got great pleasure from making toys for their children and musical instruments such as dulcimers and banjos. Most had few tools to begin with, but over the years they would accumulate a respectable collection of tools, each one extending the skill and experience the men had gained in a lifetime of making. As communities became established some men might begin to specialize, one concentrating on making wooden items, another spending his time at the forge in between his farming duties. Then they might trade bread trays for andirons. But all could boast a remarkable versatility in the creative use of their hands, and this quality added great depth to the enjoyment of life in a log cabin.

The women of log cabins were kept busy, also. There was the ancient, traditional separation of duties between the sexes, and frontier women generally fulfilled the functions women had since the prehistoric period, when log cabins were first constructed in the European northland. Their lot on the frontier was not always easy, as testified to by a young woman from Tennessee shortly after the Civil War whose new husband took her away to settle in Texas. She wrote her mother that she had found that Texas men were good to horses and hounds but hard on oxen and women!

But normally, although the work might be hard, the life was not. It was the woman's job, of course, to bear and rear the children, but this was no more difficult in a log cabin than in a city apartment, and perhaps the cabin environment offered a number of advantages. For one, cabins had yards that were filled with activities perhaps far more stimulating and educational for young children than modern electronic entertainment. There were men and women working there, and animals such as hounds, oxen, chickens, turkeys, and geese, feeding and making delightful noises.

Inside the cabin on cold or rainy days and nights there was the perpetual flame of the fire, from which young babies and toddlers were protected, and all sorts of shapes and shadows from furniture, and clothes hanging on the wall, and spinning wheels and looms. Besides, child care became easier as a family grew, for older brothers and sisters could tend to younger siblings, and if older brothers and sisters weren't around, quite often grandparents were. Diapers were no problem, for most frontier tots, and country tots until recently, ran around clad only in a shift. Problems of hygiene were easily solved with a damp rag, which would be boiled to pristine sanitariness in the next wash.

Washing was an ever-present chore, but with small families there were not too many clothes to wash, and with large families there was help. Most cabins, particularly in the South, had a special washing place adjacent to a spring or creek so that necessary water would be easily available. The washing place was equipped with rough pole racks on which to set the oak-splint baskets, generally homemade or bought from a neighbor, which were used to carry dirty clothes to the place and damp clothes back to the cabin for drying. Also there would be a rough fireplace of stone upon which would be set a large cast-iron pot in which the clothes would be boiled with lye soap. Usually, too, the washing place would have a wooden tub, perhaps half a barrel, in which to rinse the clothes, though sometimes they might be rinsed in the creek if a pool happened to be convenient. Not all cabin families enjoyed the near-godliness which cleanliness endowed, but regular weekly washing was part of living in most log cabins.

Soap, of course, like almost everything else, had to be made on the place, and soapmaking was another regular duty of the backwoods woman. Practically every cabin had its ash hopper, made by the man of the family, and mounted over a barrel. Into this the hardwood ashes were dumped whenever the hearth was cleaned. Rainwater, running through the ashes, made lye, which collected in the barrel, and lye, boiled with grease and tallow, made lye soap. Some recipes for soap yielded a hard mass that could be cut into bars, while some were for soft soap that could be ladled out of its container like cold bacon grease. Regardless of the form, however, lye soap was an excellent cleanser for clothes, although a bit hard on skin.

Gardening, both of flowers and vegetables, was usually the women's responsibility. The husband or a son generally did the plowing, for the men were more used to handling horses or oxen, but on occasion, when a man had gone to war or was sick, the women would do the plowing also, for the seasons won't wait and families must be fed, and the garden was quintessential to survival.

When a young woman married and went off with her husband to unsettled lands in the West or the South, part of her belongings included vegetable seeds carefully gathered by her mother and hoarded for the new garden. The variety in early days was limited, but it was enough to provide distinction to meals. There would be corn, of course, an American plant adopted from the Indians, as well as seeds for another American native, squash. Almost every early frontier garden included turnips, brought over from Europe, pumpkins, peas, and muskmelons. Beets, red beans, and carrots were familiar garden plants, as were cabbage and kale. In the eighteenth and early nineteenth centuries American gardens did have more different plants than those in Europe because they included both European and American staples. Later, after the world became more cosmopolitan and African influences became important in America, cabin gardens began also to include Irish potatoes, sweet potatoes, originally from South America, peanuts, and such delicacies, to some palates, as okra and collards.

Although not raised as food, gourd vines were included in most pioneer gardens. Some were of American and some of African derivation, and they made splendid bottles, bowls, and dippers, and, in the southern highlands, fiddles.

Equally prized and protected by the backwoods wife were seeds and cuttings for flower gardens. Most pioneer gardens consisted of the plants found in European gardens, such beauties as daisies, hollyhocks, and roses. But some flower gardens, even in isolated areas, had a number of far more exotic plants, many of them not remembered anymore. There was wolfsbane, for instance, with its blue or yellow blossom and poisonous root. There was asphodel from the Mediterranean and sweet William, which was native to northern Europe and Asia. There were also Coventry bells, crown imperial, and marvel of Peru. Many of the flowers of the early frontier period were cultivated for medicinal use as well as beauty.

Flowering shrubs were also represented, brought by brides who had crossed the sea from Europe and given to their daughters who set out to live in the wilderness. These, of course, were lovingly planted in the gardens of impressive plantation houses as well as some log cabins. Amazingly, some of them are occasionally still found, as living relics, growing in the deserted gardens of old cabin and house sites. Such shrubs—forgotten strains of lilacs and old roses— recall memories of France and Britain. And some reflect the continuing exploration of the world. In the late eighteenth century there were still unknown lands with many beautiful plants that found their way, through importation, to even the most isolated sections of America. Crepe myrtle and forsythia, which were imported from India about 1800, and others often brightened the yards of lonely cabins built deep in the wilderness.

Herbs, too, were the delight of pioneer women. Many of the native herbs such as queen of the meadow, ginseng, chickory, spicewood, and sassafras were adopted from the Indians. But many of the old European herbs, or yarbs as they were often called in colloquial language, were brought with the first settlers and spread along the ever-lengthening frontier. That lyrical quartet—savory, sage, rosemary, and thyme—was popular in most herb gardens of the olden days, along with yarrow, parsley, sorrel, basil, oregano, and comfrey. Some of these were obviously used to flavor foods, others were used for medicine, and still others, such as tansy, were used to keep insects out of the garden or the house.

Many cabin dwellers, of varying affluence, had a profound sense of pride in the appearance of their home places. Mr. Jim Whitley, born in his father's log cabin in Georgia in 1873, fondly recalled as a very young boy going with his elder sister to dig up cedar seedlings in the woods and planting six of them to border the path that led to the front step of the cabin. There they flourished over the years, emulating the rows of trees to the entrances of far more impressive plantation homes, until highway construction forced the eighty-year-old Whitley to leave his cabin and move into a house. Even after that, when the cabin had been moved and restored, the six sentinel cedars remained as a memorial to a pioneer family until very recently when the whole site was cleared for additional highway construction.

It would be foolish to romanticize or exaggerate the quality of life in a log cabin. Most cabin dwellers were poor and so were able to afford few luxuries and little hired help. Yet many families who spent generations in a cabin, those with pride and character, lived a good and full life, much of it because of the special qualities and atmosphere that only a one-room log cabin or a three- or four-room log house could offer. Space in a one-room cabin was certainly limited, and living conditions certainly were different from those in a large mansion, but, on the other hand, before the latter part of the nineteenth century most of the basic home activities were the same. For instance, cooking over the open fire of a one-room cabin was no different from cooking over the open fire of a saltbox house kitchen in New England or the detached kitchen with an open fire on a southern plantation. The fire was the same and the cooking equipment was generally the same.

The water supply for both a cabin and a mansion came from outside, the source being either a well or a spring. Sanitary facilities were, perforce, outside. The only real difference in living in the two types of dwelling was manifested in the appointments and the help of servants. But insofar as comfort was concerned, a log cabin woman could weave cloth as warm as that woven by servants for a rich family, and make as serviceable quilts and sew by hand clothes just as comfortable and long-lasting, albeit not so fashionable, as the clothes of rich folk.

Perhaps the main distinction of living in a log cabin was a lack of privacy. But circumstances of space simply eliminated privacy; living habits entrenched over generations and stretching back to prehistoric times made privacy of no particular importance to those who had never enjoyed it enough to give it much thought.

Several of the European and American travelers who wandered through the antebellum South and stayed overnight in log cabins, because of the absence of taverns, wrote of their impressions of cabin life. One, Edmund Kirke, a newspaperman from New York, wrote in his book, *Among the Pines* (1862), of traveling through the South just prior to the Civil War and finding overnight lodging in a cabin with a widow and her two adolescent daughters. Though there were only two beds in the cabin, he was given one and told that all three of the women would sleep in the other. He found on awakening the next morning that such a plan had not been followed. "A few streaks of grayish light were beginning to creep through the crevices in the logs, when a movement at the foot of the bed awakened me, and glancing downward I beheld the youngest girl emerging from under the clothes at my feet. She had slept there, 'cross-wise,' all night. A stir in the adjoining bed soon warned me that the other feminines were preparing to follow her example; so, turning my face to the wall, I feigned to be sleeping. Their toilet was soon made, when they quietly left Scip and myself in possession of the premises."

George R. Gilmer, who was governor of Georgia in the 1820s and 1830s, had a similar experience. Gilmer recounts in his book, *Sketches of Some of the First Settlers of Upper Georgia*, that in 1802 he and his brother were sent to attend Mr. Wilson's select classical school at Abbeville Court House, South Carolina. George was twelve years old at the time. He wrote, "Mr. Wilson put us to board with a family of Irish people, who had no children. The old man, his wife, and two nieces, the oldest a very pretty young woman, my brother and myself, slept in the same room, the cabin having but one. It was difficult, at first, to dress and undress before females."

After all, the standards of modesty in the log cabin era and in a frontier environment were entirely different from what they became when the growing affluence of America endowed almost everyone with his own room. That was an era in which as many as five or six men, all total strangers, might share a tavern or a boardinghouse bed and think nothing of it. As late as the 1850s, as recorded in the diaries of well-to-do, educated travelers, when railway passengers were forced to spend the night together in a station to transfer to another train the next day, the whole crowd prepared for bed in front of all. But then, one can read of queens being interrupted in the midst of a bath by some footman who could not reach another room in the unpassaged palace of Versailles without going through the queen's bathroom. Modesty was there, but it was frequently forced aside for practical reasons, and no one thought much about it. Attitudes were different in those times, and such attitudes persisted longer in log cabins. Sometimes quilts or blankets might be hung from the ceiling joists to give a measure of privacy, but usually privacy was not that important.

So, if one is to develop an understanding of log cabin living, the crowdedness, or coziness, of cabin life must be faced. In reality it was a rather dramatic life in which one was exposed naturally to birth and death, sickness and joy, sadness and pleasure, and, especially on the frontier, danger from Indian attack. All of this happened in a one-room cabin, and all the dwellers in that cabin shared it, emotionally and physically. Cabin living was an education in life as a whole.

Generally, it was a good life that most cabin dwellers enjoyed, perhaps because of the varied experiences that were concentrated in one small enclosed area isolated in the vast woodlands.

There were sounds, for one thing, sounds quite different from the roar of traffic, of electronic devices, or of electrically driven appliances. The sounds of a cabin were purposeful sounds: a baby crying and the plaintive lullaby to quiet the crying, the regular rhythm and gentle whining of a spinning wheel before the fire at night offering the promise of security and warmth, the muted thumping of the loom.

There was the continual, always different music of the fire: poppings and hissings and bumpings as a log burned in two and fell into the bed of glowing coals. The noises of the fire might be accompanied by the tantalizing sound of a pot of food boiling or a joint of meat sizzling over the coals. When a spider was pulled from the fire its iron legs scraped over the hearthstone, and when the crane was moved it often gave a barely heard squeak. At night the women prepared food and the men repaired equipment, and each of these tasks generated its own identifiable sounds.

Sometimes, when no chore pressed too hard, men or women would play the fiddle or pluck the gentle dulcimer or pick a guitar or banjo for the sheer joy of controlling the melody or harmony of a tune or ballad.

In the wintertime the wall logs might almost talk when freezing weather made them contract and the corner joints settled, and complaining noises were the result. In the summertime the sound of rain on the shingled roof provided its own lullaby to those who had worked hard all day in field or forest.

A background to this symphony of domestic sounds was the human voice in all its manifestations. Men and older boys would bring in news from other settlements where they had taken a raft of logs to a mill. The women might relate gossip they had heard from a passing peddler, and the old people would respond by telling of some long-ago incident that had happed to them. Then there were stories from time to time, some of them folk tales, some read from the Bible, and some true stories and news from more populated areas related by an overnight guest.

Outside, from faraway, one might hear the hooting of an owl, the bark of a fox, or the harmonious baying of hounds running a bear. From the barn would come the occasional lowing of cattle or the agitated cackling of chickens threatened by a weasel.

Of all the features of a cabin, however, the eternal fire was perhaps the most thought-provoking. For each cabin was a small universe and the fire was the sun of that universe. It usually burned day and night, winter and summer, fall and spring, for its main function was for cooking, and, besides, in the days before matches, starting a fire was something of a chore. Indeed, Bryan Owle, reared in a cabin on Goose Creek on the Cherokee Reservation in North Carolina, remembered, as a boy in the early twentieth century, being awakened fairly frequently by a Cherokee who lived up the creek, coming to borrow a pan of hot coals to rekindle his fire because he had no matches.

Every log cabin dweller, old and young, male and female, white man or Indian, was an expert in building and maintaining fires. A fire for cooking was maintained in one way to provide a minimum of flames but a fine bed of hot coals. Fires for heating were maintained in another manner, and fires for giving light in still another. But whether a fire was good or bad for any of these uses depended on factors other than how the logs were stacked. The type of wood used was of basic importance.

There were varied preferences in firewood based on longevity, fragrance, and the amount of light a wood would produce when aflame. Accessibility, too, was always a factor.

Some firemakers swore by beech, even though it was hard to split. Others chose oak because it made a fine, hot fire and good coals and was quite easy to split. Still others who lived in settled communities would avidly seek out applewood with its unsurpassed fragrance and beautiful white ash. But most, in areas where it was readily available, swore by hickory, some disdaining all but green hickory.

There were good reasons for thinking hickory the premier firewood of the world, dry or green. Hickory burned longer than other woods and put out more heat per cubic foot. It was relatively easy to split and caught easily with a minimum of kindling. Hickory made a pretty fire, its flames ranging from blue to orange to bright yellow. It had a rather acrid aroma when burning that gave a subtle perfume to the whole room.

Green hickory multiplied all those qualities. It burned longer and hotter than dry wood, gave off more fragrance, and sizzled as jets of steam issued from the end grain of the logs. Once burned, the coals of green hickory lasted a day or two if banked with an inch or so of gray ash. Those who had made fires of green hickory could be assured of a hot bed of coals when they arose in the morning because, when fanned with a turkey wing, the coals would light new pine kindling almost immediately.

Pine was used as firewood sometimes, but usually only to kindle a fire. It caught quickly, but it also burned quickly. It took twice as many pine logs to last an evening as it did hickory or oak or beech. Of course, "lightard" wood, the resin-impregnated splinters from pine stumps or knots in fallen trees, was the supreme kindling, catching as soon as it was touched by a match, giving off a black, oily smoke and an aromatic, cleansing odor. Many cabins kept a basketful of pine knots by the fire so that when light was needed a knot could be thrown on the coals. In a moment it would explode with a bright flame that lighted up the room quite as effectively as candles or lamps and far better than a rushlight. According to legend, young Abraham Lincoln used to lie on the hearthstone reading precious books by the light of pine knots.

There were some woods, mostly of the resinous varieties, that were anathema as firewood or kindling. Spruce, balsam, and particularly hemlock were filled with tiny knots and pockets of air that popped viciously when the wood was burning, scattering ashes and hot coals to a distance of three or four feet at times and creating a fire hazard that was intolerable in a log cabin.

Those who lived in log cabins became fire virtuosos, even fire worshipers of sorts, because of the elemental importance of fire in almost every aspect of life. A fire in the hearth was always there, a real part of life, repaying the massive effort of cutting and stacking firewood to replenish the flames day after day. But aside from the creature comforts a fire provided, it also was a source of aesthetic pleasure or entertainment. A fire was a mobile painting when the flames leaped up dancing between the logs; a source of mystery when a pocket of gas within a log was released and burned inches above the other flames; a source that could be controlled by judicious poking and pulling to adjust the flow of hot air rising between the logs, thus creating proper draft for any desired intensity. Fires were centers of fascination, each constantly changing, each different, each one beautiful.

The Hoosier poet, James Whitcomb Riley, who was reared in a log cabin in Greenfield, Indiana, touched on this fascination in his poem "Little Orphant Annie." In this excerpt he describes the indentured orphan servant girl entertaining the children of the house by telling ghost stories in front of the kitchen hearth:

> *We set around the kitchen fire an' has the mostest fun*
> *A-listening to the witch-tales 'at Annie tells about,*
> *An' the Gobble-uns -at gits you*
> *Ef you Don't Watch Out!*
>
> *An' little Orphant Annie says, when the blaze is blue,*
> *An' the lamp wick sputters, an' the wind goes woo-oo!*
> *An' you hear the crickets quit, an' the moon is gray,*
> *An' the lightnin'-bugs in dew is all squenched away—*
> *You better mind yer parunts, an' yer teachers fond an' dear,*
> *An' churish them 'at loves you, an' dry the orphant's tear,*
> *An' hep the pore an' needy ones 'at clusters all about,*
> *Er the Gobble-uns 'll git you Ef you Don't Watch Out!*

Families that were born and reared in the log cabins of early America lived a crowded life, but usually a good one. Those who remembered childhood days usually recounted pleasant memories, experiences that had shaped their characters, and an awareness of the world that would not have been quite so sharp had they lived in another place.

Most had a deeply ingrained sense of self-reliance, a self-sufficiency that could not have been drawn from any home but a log cabin.

PART TWO

THE LOG CABIN PRESERVED

ONCE log buildings were so much a part of the rural landscape in most areas of the country that everyone took them for granted. All of a sudden, in the middle of the twentieth century, log cabins seemed to disappear almost completely.

In the 1950s huge earth-moving machines, products of the technology developed during World War II, began to cut large swaths across the American landscape, and fertile bottomland was replaced by concrete and asphalt highways. The buildings that had been part of this terrain vanished along with the fields.

Even where farmland was left intact, there were other modernizing trends to contend with. Farm laborers, whose jobs had been taken over by the new farm machines, poured into the burgeoning cities of America with their families, abandoning unneeded farm buildings. Those who remained on the farms were introduced to the delights of modern plumbing, modern stoves, and other conveniences, while improved roads enabled them to achieve a new affluence. Farm people began moving into modern houses, building steel shelters for their farm machines. The old rural America was disappearing forever.

More than just physical structures, log cabins are symbolic of an American ideal. They evoke memories of a time when family privacy and personal identity and loyal relationships were still an integral part of American life. Though so many log buildings are gone, they will not—and should not—be forgotten. Fortunately, a growing number of log cabins and houses, some privately owned and some owned by historical societies, are being preserved and lovingly restored.

In this section of the book, which we have called The Log Cabin Preserved, we have tried to create a kind of picture album of some of the best remaining examples of log structures in different parts of the United States and Canada, trying to include not only log homes but also log barns, corncribs, and other structures built in a variety of styles and with a variety of construction methods. Most of the places photographed and described here are from the Appalachian region, for that is where the majority of the best-preserved examples in America are to be found. In this region there are still people who actually continue to live in old, classically constructed cabins of hand-hewn logs. Such families are few, indeed, however, and even in that last stronghold of cabins, the Qualla Indian Reservation in North Carolina, where log cabins were being built up until the 1950s, families have abandoned them for mobile homes with enclosed baths and shiny kitchens.

More and more beautiful log structures are being discovered and preserved or restored everywhere. Throughout the South particularly, and in Maryland, Delaware, Pennsylvania, and Tennessee, many fine old houses in rural areas, or in what once were rural areas, are discovered to be hiding a log cabin behind their carefully painted weatherboarding. In a fashionable and affluent neighborhood in Atlanta, for example, there is a house, the core of which is a log cabin built in 1823 in the midst of virgin forest only recently abandoned by Creek Indians. The house has never been moved, and those who pass by and admire it could never guess that the main structure is made of notched logs, with additions that date back a century and a half.

Probably many of the kitchens, or what once were detached kitchens, of stately mansions in Virginia and North Carolina, South Carolina, and Georgia, are of logs neatly covered by clapboards. It was a custom in the years when the country was being settled for a man to convert his original log home into a kitchen when he had the funds to build his real "dream" house.

There are many more fine examples of log cabins to be found in the East and the West of this country as well as in Canada. It was impossible to include more than a representative sampling of the many outstanding examples of log cabins and houses, but it is our hope that with the publication of this book more people will learn about the old and venerable tradition of log cabin building and be proud to contribute to the further preservation of log buildings everywhere.

DURST HOUSE
Atlanta, Georgia

Relocated and restored behind the house of Mr. and Mrs. William Durst in northwest Atlanta, this splendid, carefully crafted log house could well have been raised in the late eighteenth century. It was built near Roberta, Georgia, on the old Oakfuskee Indian Trail, a trading artery that ran from Charleston to New Orleans.

Flat notching was used on the Durst House. Nail holes in the wall suggest that the cabin was at one time covered with clapboards. The wide interstices between the logs of this well-built structure support this theory. These "cracks" were sometimes intended for the insertion of nogging, masonry comprised of bricks and mud. Nogging provided both strength and insulation, and it was effective in stopping Indian bullets as well. The use of nogging was widespread in the late eighteenth century in England and America, for both log and frame houses.

Above: A back view of the Durst restoration in Atlanta. The house apparently had two back doors, an unusual design. The picture shows that one door has been converted into a window and its lower part closed off by sawn boards.

Left: Further evidence of the early origins of this building is in the shaping and fitting of the top logs on its front and back and sides. The side logs extend over front and back while staying flush with the rest of the wall. Front and back logs, however, overlap those underneath in a rather sophisticated manner. Also, the insides of the front and back top logs are flush with the interior walls in the top half-story.

Above: The Durst House has an unusually high hearth front in its living room and no mantelpiece. It is likely that its original interior walls were covered with paneling or plaster, although the nicely hewn logs are most decorative in the restoration.

Right: Unlike most frontier cabins, this structure is divided by a plank wall into two rooms. The elegant narrow stairway, found in finer cabins of this period, leads to a commodious loft.

JOHN ROSS HOUSE
Rossville, Georgia

The restored log house in Rossville, Georgia (formerly Ross's Landing), where John Ross, the elective chief of the Cherokee Nation, once lived in relative splendor. The son of a wealthy Scotch trader, Ross was only one-eighth Indian, but in the matriarchal tradition of his tribe he was considered a Cherokee because his Indian blood was on his mother's side. The house was originally raised around 1790 and was moved and restored by the D.A.R. in the 1930s, when it was about to be torn down to make way for a service station. Although the cut-stone chimneys, the porch railing, and the sawn-shingle roof are of questionable authenticity, the majesty of the restored building is undoubtedly retained from the original proportions. The Ross House is of two-crib, two-story design, with a spacious dogtrot on the first floor and an enclosed hallway on the second. The enclosing wall on the hallway is unusual—it is constructed of logs that are notched and fitted into the wall logs. An oblique view of the building, above, shows its front and rear porches and, typical of the eighteenth century, the low angle of the roof gable. What has been restored is only the log frame of the structure that was covered by clapboards (see page 17).

FORT YARGO
near Winder, Georgia

Fort Yargo, pictured above left on its original site near Winder, Georgia, has an interesting history. Built under government contract by the Humphries brothers in 1792, the structure is one of a group of four blockhouses put up to meet a threatened uprising of Creek and Cherokee Indians along the Georgia frontier. It was originally accompanied by a spring at a distance of only one hundred feet, and both spring and blockhouse were enclosed within a log stockade. The Indian war never materialized, and when Fort Yargo was sold in 1810 to John Hill for use as a private residence, its stockade was torn down. The building remained in private ownership as late as the 1950s and was used as a farm storage house. It is now in use as part of a state park for elderly citizens. Remarkably, very little restoration was required to bring Fort Yargo to its current fine condition.

The view of Fort Yargo, on the above right, reveals the structure's fine fieldstone chimney and the small window, which was doubtless intended for a rifle port, in the second half-story. As befits a military building, rifle ports were cut into the walls, shown in the picture below right, one above the door and one beside it. The circular saw marks on the boards of the door and door frames are evidence that these components are replacements.

BRANNON CABIN
Wilkinson County, Georgia

Built in 1821 by Adam Brannon in Wilkinson County, Georgia, this cabin was larger than most of its contemporaries. The generous proportions of its central room, measuring twenty-eight by twenty feet, reflect the availability of virgin longleaf pine in that area, just eighteen miles south of Milledgeville, then the capital of Georgia. Another distinction of the Brannon Cabin is its parson's room, usually found in larger and more sophisticated frame houses. This furnished room, located at one end of the front porch, offered accommodations to the circuit preacher who found himself without lodgings for the night. He could settle into a bed in the parson's room without waking the family. Moved from its original site and carefully restored by the Paul Hawkins family, the cabin now serves as a weekend retreat at Big Canoe, a resort area north of Atlanta, Georgia. While the outside dimensions of the structure and its porches have not been changed, the Hawkinses have transformed this well-built antique cabin into a comfortable two-bedroom residence with all the modern conveniences.

TOM WATSON BIRTHPLACE
McDuffie County, Georgia

Above: A rear view of the house where the fiery populist Tom Watson was born. The house was built by Watson's grandfather in McDuffie County, Georgia, in about 1820. Watson, who was best known for establishing Rural Free Delivery when he was a U.S. Congressman (1891–1893) was a very fine writer. He described his birthplace in an autobiographical novel:

"Ours was just a plain house and none too large, not built of bricks brought over from England, but of timbers torn from the heart of the longleaf Georgia pine.

"The main body was made of logs hewed with the broad-axe, smoothed with the footadze, and joined powerfully at the ends—the four corners—by being interlocked into deep notches; upon these solid, heavy logs was laid, inside and out, a covering of plank: strong sleepers bore up the plank floor, stout rafters held the shingle roof. A partition, running from side to side nearest the western end, cut the main body of the original house into two parts, the smaller being a bedroom, the larger being the living room, where life on the homestead centered. Two stone chimneys, built outside, gave fireplaces to the living room and to the shed room. The house rested upon massive stone piers, two feet high, well-set in the ground . . .

"Such was my grandfather's house built for comfort, built to resist the storms of a hundred years . . .

"That old Southern homestead was a little kingdom, a complete social and industrial organism, almost wholly sufficient unto itself, asking less of the outer world than it gave."

Tom Watson ran unsuccessfully for president in 1900 as candidate of the People's party. He used his birthplace of logs as one of his appeals, following in the tradition of Andrew Jackson, Henry Clay, and William Henry Harrison.

Left: The living room fireplace of the Watson House. Ceiling joists can be seen above. The fire brick is probably not original, for in most old cabins fireplaces were lined with plain brick or stone.

A front view of the Tom Watson birthplace in McDuffie County,
Georgia. The house, which is in the typical form of a frontier log cabin, is
covered by clapboards that have been nailed onto massive logs. The
structure was moved sixteen miles from its original site and restored
in 1975.

CREEK INDIAN AGENCY CABIN
Monroe County, Georgia

This typical English-type cabin is still on its original site on a bluff overlooking the former Creek Indian Agency on the Oconee River in Monroe County, Georgia. Since the Creeks in this area were removed between 1825 and 1830, it is likely that the cabin was built during the 1820s. The end wall was later mutilated to install an additional door and adapt the building to farm storage. The chimney has disappeared, leaving its vacant opening in the opposite wall. According to local tales, this structure was originally a blockhouse, but the evidence suggests it was a dwelling. Mortises in the lintel log on the right show where porch rafters were once placed. The two auger holes midway up the side wall indicate that a weaver once lived in this cabin. Pegs were placed in the holes and used to wind yarn after dyeing or spinning.

VANN CABIN
Chatsworth, Georgia

An atypical cabin of extraordinary workmanship, **which stands behind the Vann House, home** of a wealthy Cherokee chief at Chatsworth, Georgia. The cabin was used as an office and servants' quarters. Although of logs, usually considered a rather unsophisticated building material, this well-made structure fits in very well with the fine brick residence that was built about 1800 by Vann slaves and fine European craftsmen. The full dovetail notching indicates German influence, which would fit the tradition of the Vann place. Chief James Vann, though a pagan, invited Moravian missionaries to settle on his place about 1801, donating land for dwellings and a school. His purpose was not to save the souls of his tribesmen but to teach them blacksmithing, weaving, reading and writing, and efficient agricultural methods. Several of the Moravian families emigrated to the Cherokee Nation from Salem, North Carolina. The structure in this photograph closely resembles some of the log town houses still standing at Old Salem today. The screens on door and windows are, of course, an anachronism.

NEW ECHOTA RESTORATION

Calhoun, Georgia

Below: A view of the partially restored Cherokee capital of New Echota on the bottom-land plain of the Oostanaula River near Calhoun, Georgia. The building in the foreground is the print shop, unique among Indian nations of the early nineteenth century. In the background stands Vann's Store, which also served as a tavern. New Echota, founded in 1825 and named for the ancient sanctuary village of Echota in Tennessee, was a bustling town until the tragic Removal of the highly civilized and cultured Cherokees in 1839.

Above: The print shop is an elegant reproduction of the earlier log building. Pieces of type used in printing the *Cherokee Phoenix*, the national newspaper, which was half in English and half in Cherokee, were discovered here and offer archaeological evidence that the shop stands on its original site. The Cherokees are the only American Indians who had their own alphabet or syllabary, invented by the genius Sequoyah, a cripple who never went to school and never learned to speak English.

Left: The fine craftsmanship of these nicely chamfered porch posts and well-joined railings and benches undoubtedly reflects Moravian influence. Moravian missionaries settled among the Cherokees at the invitation of Chief Joseph Vann, a pagan, in 1800. The well-proportioned windows provide light for the type cases on one side of the interior and for the Franklin printing press on the other side.

Vann's Store, or Vann's Tavern, at the New Echota Restoration near Calhoun, Georgia, was built in 1800 and originally situated near Oscarville, Georgia, an area that was ceded by the Cherokees in 1819. The building was moved in the 1950s to its present site. The structure and details of the two-story log section are authentic. However, the vertical board and batten weatherboarding of the wing to the left may be anachronistic. This feature is generally seen in houses built after 1850, and New Echota was destroyed eleven years earlier, at the time of the Cherokee Removal.

The corner notches on the Cherokee print shop, an example of fine joinery. The offset notch in the sill log is an unusual refinement, reflecting the probable influence of Moravian missionaries on the buildings at New Echota. This kind of joint provided considerably more strength than the typical flat notch, which was frequently used to join lower logs and sills.

Constructed of hewn, notched, and pegged timbers, the Vann's Tavern well-shed is interesting because of its unusual log well curb and its typical watering trough, which was made from a hollow log.

The half-dovetail joints on the tavern indicate that the builder was English. Scotch-Irish settlers usually relied on saddle notching. The position of the sill log is unusual in that it rests under a side wall rather than a front or back wall. Also, the sill is half dovetailed instead of joined by the usual square notch found on most sills. The porch sills are joined by a square notch.

Access to the guest quarters at Vann's Tavern, at the New Echota
Restoration, near Calhoun, Georgia, was by an outside rear stairway. The
second story was composed of one large room furnished with several beds,
which could accommodate as many as five weary travelers each, a custom
in backwoods Georgia taverns in the early nineteenth century. The well was
dug close to the tavern for the convenience of guests, cooks, and beasts.

Vann's Tavern, like many frontier taverns, was not a place for
entertainment so much as a source of supplies. The small window to the
left of the back door is said to have been installed so that bottles of whiskey
could be passed out to customers who were not guests in the tavern.

LIBRARY CABIN
Lumpkin, Georgia

The town of Lumpkin, Georgia, uses a beautifully crafted restored dogtrot cabin for its library. The claim of some authorities that the dogtrot design did not originate until about 1825 can be disputed. House plans featuring a hallway with one or two rooms on each side and chimneys at both ends could be found in England and America in the early eighteenth century. George Washington's Mount Vernon follows essentially the same floor plan for its two stories. Mount Vernon was started as a one-story house around 1760.

Left: Careful examination reveals that the Lumpkin Library once had its elegantly hewn logs covered with weatherboarding. Inside the dogtrot one can see where the logs were hewn to true vertical furring strips on which clapboards or weatherboarding were nailed. Also, the intentionally wide interstices between the logs for brick and mud nogging and the square notches, instead of saddle or half-dovetail, are both signs that the log pen was built to substitute for the mortised and pegged frame that was common in clapboard houses before about 1840.

ABANDONED HOUSE
Concord, Georgia

Very little is known about this abandoned double-pen house, shown above left, which stands in a field near Concord, Georgia. The small chimneys of half fieldstone and half brick fix the structure's origins before 1840. From the outside the building appears to be barely more than a neglected tenement, but on closer examination of its deteriorated front and inside walls the secret of its construction is revealed.

The exterior weatherboarding with butted, rather than overlapping edges, suggests that the house dates from the early nineteenth or possibly late eighteenth century. In the picture above right, where neglect has allowed missing weatherboarding to go unrepaired, a solid frame of finely hewn logs is revealed beneath the building's skin, the vertical furring for nailing weatherboarding still intact. This plainly is not just another backwoods log cabin later furnished with a cosmetic skin and made to look like a fashionable frame house. The log core was built to substitute as a frame, with corners fitted so that the interstices between the logs would be nearly nonexistent. Chinking and nogging were unnecessary—careful hewing and fitting made this frame into a nearly solid box.

The inside walls of the house, below , are truer to their origins than the exterior. These nicely hewn logs have apparently never been hidden by either boards or plaster. The cracks between the logs were covered with long furring strips to make the structure draft-proof. The result makes the room look as if it's been paneled with horizontal hewn boards.

WESTVILLE RESTORATION

outside Lumpkin, Georgia

The Welles House, a commodious two-story frame house in the process of being restored at Westville, a restoration village outside Lumpkin, Georgia. The original building, a one-room log cabin built by a Creek Indian prior to 1817, was virtually absorbed by the frame structure of the house built around 1825. The Welles family is said to have lived in the Indian cabin after the Creek Removal in 1825, while the frame addition was being constructed. Now a ground-floor room with its own door and two added windows shown to the left of the main entrance, the cabin is built of split twelve-inch logs of longleaf pine, which were hewn into planks only about four inches thick.

Archaeologists have deduced from the notches cut into the upper wall logs that the original Indian inhabitants installed a sleeping platform—not restored when the photograph at left was taken—several feet off the floor in front of the fireplace. Sleeping platforms were common in the prehistoric housing of most of the eastern Woodlands tribes, from New England to Florida.

Right: At the farmhouse of the Westville Restoration, near Lumpkin, Georgia, the kitchen is a separate building attached to the house by a breezeway, as was customary in most farms between 1700 and 1850. The massive chimney shows that the fireplace was used for cooking rather than heating.

Below: The cornfield behind the farmhouse exhibits typical frontier farming methods. Corn was planted around the stumps of trees cut for logs, which were left in the field until they rotted away. On occasion, if logs were not needed for buildings or fences, trees were bridled by cutting away a strip of bark around the circumference of the trunk. This, of course, killed the tree and allowed sunlight to reach the corn. Bridled trees could then be cleared at the settler's leisure and used for firewood and for other materials.

Left: Built in 1840 four miles south of Stockbridge, Georgia, as a home for the Dabney family, this English-style cabin is presently situated at Westville. There was little difference in the styles of north Georgia and south Georgia cabins at the time the Dabney House was raised. Indeed, when all Indian lands in Georgia became available for settlement between 1820 and 1840, the state drew new citizens, and, coming from as far north as Pennsylvania and as close as adjacent South Carolina, these people often shared a common tradition of cabin building.

In frontier farms and large plantations alike, a room or space somewhere in the main house was usually devoted to weaving. This loom at the farmhouse is being used to weave a colorful cotton bed coverlet. Most often two strips were sewn together to make coverlets wide enough for beds that accommodated two adults and even more children.

Above: Saddlebag cabins—those with a single divided crib and usually with a central chimney—are rather rare. The interior of this saddlebag cabin at the Westville Restoration outside Lumpkin, Georgia, has been altered to serve as a pottery shop. The ends of the log wall that divided the interior can be seen projecting out between the two doors.

Left: Backwoods craftsmen in early America, as in Europe, practiced their crafts at their homes. Here, the potter's homemade, wood-fired kiln is only a short distance from his home.

LEVERETT CABIN
Smyrna, Georgia

This small, nicely proportioned building is a fine example of the most beautiful type of log cabin—those built of tulip poplar logs. The building was initially constructed, without windows, of split trunks hewn to boards about six inches thick. Some of the lower logs are over two feet wide. Moved from its original site in Gilmer County, Georgia, and restored by Charles Poss in Smyrna, the cabin is thought to have been built in 1839 by a man named Duncan Leverett. However, the English-style proportions and the log gable ends with pole purlins, as well as the low roof, make this structure typical of earlier cabins. The roof was probably once of log shakes instead of shingles as the distance between the purlins would suggest. A window was cut in the opposite end of the building by one of the families that lived here. Even the temporary asbestos roof in this picture cannot take away from the beauty of the building's proportions. Legend has it that in over two generations twenty-one children were reared in this tiny house, some mere sixteen by sixteen feet in dimension, with at least nine people living here at one time.

Where sawn lumber was hard to come by, pole purlins were used instead of boards. Emplaced without nails, the purlins rested in notches in the retrogressing logs of the gables. The cabin was probably originally roofed with split shakes, which were larger than shingles. The shakes would have been secured by poles placed over them and tied to the purlins, thus making it possible to complete a cabin without the use of a single nail.

Poplar logs were so large that they were usually split before hewing to provide perfectly matched courses in opposite walls. Because green poplar is soft and easily hewn the half-logs could be dressed into planks no more than four inches thick, making them lighter in weight and easier to lift for the top courses. Logically the largest logs were used for the bottom of the walls and smaller, lighter logs for the upper portions.

SIBLEY CABIN
Roswell, Georgia

Above: A log cabin on its original site in the Sweet Apple community near Roswell. Built around 1850 as a home, the building remained in use as a one-room school until the 1920s. The present owner and resident is Celestine Sibley, a writer who has had a long love affair with log cabins. The structure is entirely without chinking—the gaps are closed on the interior by horizontal boards. Legend has it that the boards were once removed in the warm weather to allow more light for the scholars at work inside. On the left is a recent addition, another cabin moved from several miles away and restored to provide more living and working space.

Left: An unusual corncrib behind the Sibley Cabin. The roof is not original but rests on a frame that enabled the original roof to open like a divided box top, making it easier to load corn in the crib from the top. The mortised purlins in the roof frame indicate that shakes were used for roofing. Top logs, front and back, were left protruding and notched on top to provide a pivot for the roof frame. The crib was raised in Cherokee County, Georgia, probably during the 1840s, after the Indians had been removed. The extended gable and the building's proportions suggest German influence.

WOOD-RAIFORD HOUSE
outside Roswell, Georgia

This fine story-and-a-half cabin, shown in the process of restoration, is now the home of Judy Wood-Raiford and Jere Wood outside of Roswell, Georgia. It was moved to its present site from Cherokee County, Georgia. Its fieldstone chimney is particularly well restored. Since this photograph was taken, a plank kitchen has been added and the second half-story made into an attractive bedroom suite. The front windows were undoubtedly installed long after the cabin was built, which was probably around 1850. The doors in early cabins were left open in all seasons to do double duty as windows.

STONE MOUNTAIN PARK CABIN

near Atlanta, Georgia

Simple but well made and nicely proportioned, this restored cabin at Stone Mountain Park is typical of log cabins in the South during the nineteenth century.

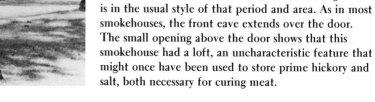

The smokehouse, or meat house, behind the log cabin is in the usual style of that period and area. As in most smokehouses, the front eave extends over the door. The small opening above the door shows that this smokehouse had a loft, an uncharacteristic feature that might once have been used to store prime hickory and salt, both necessary for curing meat.

ISAAC HILL HOUSE

Callaway Gardens, Georgia

This story-and-a-half house was built by or for Isaac Hill around 1800 in Troup County, Georgia. Troup County was named for General Troup, who was the first Indian agent for the "Five Civilized Tribes of the Southeast." At the time, Georgia extended to the Mississippi River and included what are now the states of Alabama and Mississippi. Hill must have been either a trader or in the employ of General Troup because there was no legal white settlement in that area in 1800. His house shows signs of having been weatherboarded at one time. The windows are thought to have been included in the early structure and enlarged several generations later. This house was occupied continually from 1800 to 1936. It was moved from its original site in 1959 to Callaway Gardens, a twenty-five-hundred-acre recreational resort, just a few miles from where the Hill House stood for a hundred and fifty-nine years.

Above: Undoubtedly original and of original size, this small window in the Isaac Hill House at Callaway Gardens, Georgia, is neatly set into the end-wall logs next to the chimney. Braced shutters were typical of most cabins, but glazing usually indicated an uncommon affluence. The corner notching on this house is deep enough to almost eliminate the need for chinking between the logs.

Left: The original smokehouse, or meat house, which is quite close to the main house, was also moved to its present location in 1959. Built of massive hewn logs with German-style overhanging eaves in front, this structure has the removable floorboards typical for its kind. When the boards were taken up, a smoldering fire of hickory could be lighted on the earthen underfloor enabling the meat hanging from the rafters to be cured.

A snug corner of the main room. The inside walls have been whitewashed, a practice frequently used to reflect and increase the light from windows and open doors. The Hill House had more luxurious and tasteful furniture than most frontier log cabins.

Nicely made of brick and stucco, the hearth displays accouterments that were often found in early log cabins. The tin candlesticks might have been bought from a traveling tinker. Tree forks as well as antlers were placed over the fireplace for gun racks, though they were never used together as shown here and never for so feminine a tool as a sedge broom.

The well-shed, replaced in its original juxtaposition to the Isaac Hill House, at Callaway Gardens, Georgia, was handy to both the house and the kitchen, which was not replaced. The barns would also have been fairly close to the well, so that the animals could be watered without too much difficulty.

TULLIE SMITH HOUSE RESTORATION
Atlanta, Georgia

A fine restored corncrib, of two-crib design, at the Tullie Smith House Restoration on the grounds of the Atlanta Historical Society. The left crib is eight logs high and the right is of a height of only seven logs, so that the whole building fits into the slope of the ground and the roof remains level. The structure originally stood in northern Georgia in an area with many sawmills, and its shingles have been sawn rather than split. The vertical planks on the gable ends indicate that the corncrib was erected, or perhaps modified, after 1850.

A massive one-crib barn at the Tullie Smith House Restoration in Atlanta. Most log buildings of this size usually encompassed two cribs covered by a common roof. This photograph shows the rear of the barn and the access to the hayloft. Joists for the loft floor are mortised into a wall log and can be seen protruding slightly. The sill rests on simple piers made of fieldstone.

The Slave Cabin at the Tullie Smith House Restoration on the grounds of the Atlanta Historical Society. In 1830 when the Smith House was raised, its builder owned seventeen slaves on his farm in DeKalb County, Georgia, and this building, which now serves as a gift shop at the Restoration, has been designated the Slave Cabin. It is typical of many rural dwellings in northern Georgia during the 1830s and 1840s. The small, unglazed window is closed by a wooden shutter, a feature that, along with the horizontal weatherboarding on the gable ends, marks this as a pre-Industrial Age cabin. The unpeeled yellow poplar porch posts are also characteristic of cabins of this period.

A front view of the barn and the post and rail fence enclosing the barnyard, which would be quite sturdy enough to restrict even the strongest bull or most independent mule. In the English farm tradition, the wicket-type gate has strap hinges with ball finials. Strap hinges are thought to have originated with the Viking invaders of England in the ninth century. The Norse strap hinge depicted a legendary dragon which supposedly afforded supernatural protection against thieves and other intruders.

This end view of the Tullie Smith House Restoration barn in Atlanta, Georgia, shows how the logs for this building were joined. The construction method— joining the logs for an interior wall by fitting them into the center of the end-wall logs—was unusual. Most interior divisions in log buildings were made of pole and plank. The floor joists of the hayloft can be seen protruding from the side walls.

The Tullie Smith House Restoration barn exhibits several interesting features. The latch on the door to the animal stalls, shown at left, is no more than a peg struck across the door edge into an oblique auger hole, a simple but wholly functional closure. The door, however, is a replacement, as indicated by the circular saw marks, which were not known before 1850, ten years or so after the barn was built. The door to the toolroom, shown below left, has a handmade iron hasp with an iron pin. Staples were long enough to be clinched on the other side of door and jamb. Extra security could be obtained by substituting a padlock for the iron pin.

The spacious interior of the Tullie Smith House Restoration barn, pictured below, is subdivided by a log wall into storage space in the rear and animal stalls in the front with access to the barnyard. Log barns were almost never chinked, but the shingle or shake roofs gave excellent protection from rain or snow and the huge wall logs provided a great deal of protection from the wind. The loft, of course, was used for hay storage.

JIM WHITLEY CABIN
Atlanta, Georgia

The Jim Whitley Cabin, built in 1842 in the upper settlement of Vinings, Georgia, was moved to Atlanta for restoration. It is a fine example of a typical Scotch-Irish design, with opposing front and rear doors. Mr. Whitley was born in this cabin, which was built by his grandfather, and remained here until shortly before his death when a new highway forced him to move. Every spring Mr. Whitley checked and renewed the chinking with red clay. When the roof began to deteriorate in the 1950s, he cut a white oak board tree in a patch of virgin woods on his forty-acre farm, rived shingles, and replaced the roof. The original roof was rather low, in the style of the 1840s, but Mr. Whitley's replacement was higher. When the cabin was moved, the original rafters were found in the loft, which was reached by a ladder in one corner of the room. This cabin had a root cellar, which Mr. Whitley used as his refrigerator.

The stone masonry in the chimney of the Whitley Cabin is truly classic. Mr. Whitley related that his grandfather and father, with help from neighbors, built the cabin, but they called in the master mason in the community to lay the fieldstone chimney. The lean-to attached to the cabin was built by Mr. Whitley in the 1920s for use as a kitchen. In practice, though, he did most of his cooking over the fire, as his mother and grandmother had done before him.

Above: The end wall of the Jim Whitley Cabin before it was moved to Atlanta and restored. This picture gives a good view of the original dry wall foundation and shows the door to the root cellar. Vertical gable end boards are atypical of construction styles at the time the cabin was built. They were installed by Mr. Whitley when he modified the roof angle in the 1920s.

Left: Another view of the chimney, which also reveals the dry wall construction of the original foundation and the oaken sill log. When first built, the window was small and unglazed. Mr. Whitley enlarged and glazed it during the 1920s.

An interior view of the cabin after restoration. The chairs were the homemade type that either Mr. Whitley or his father would have made. A bar set into the back of the hearth from which cooking utensils were suspended by pothooks was used instead of a crane for cooking. A traditional turkey wing could serve to fan the fire when needed.

The Whitley Cabin as restored when relocated to the rear of a house in northwest Atlanta. Fortunately the new owner was able to preserve part of the feeling of the original construction by using authentic split shingles of white oak for the roof.

A view of the cabin after one of the rare snowfalls in the Atlanta area. The frosting of white snow shows why log cabins may be considered the native architecture of the American wilderness: they blend perfectly with their settings regardless of the season.

KELLY CABIN

Rossville, Georgia

The Kelly Cabin, standing on its original site in Rossville, Georgia, at the Chickamauga and Chattanooga National Military Park, which spans northern Georgia and Tennessee. During the Battle of Chickamauga in 1863, this cabin was the center of a bloody conflict between Union and Confederate forces and bears the scars of minié balls in its logs. The Kelly Cabin sills rest on the ground without either foundation or piers; this is unusual. The log hearth and chimney, lined with clay, suggests that the structure was built in the 1840s, shortly after the Cherokees were removed from northern Georgia. An overhanging gable protects the chimney and its chinking from damage by rain.

The front view of the cabin shows the protruding floor and ceiling joists. The ceiling and door are much lower than was usual in later cabins. Typical of Scotch-Irish design, the cabin is somewhat rectangular, with opposite doors, front and rear, and no windows. Daytime lighting came from open doors, both summer and winter.

HOOKS CABIN

near Tifton, Georgia

Still standing where it was originally built for the Hooks family in the 1890s, this superb example of a latter-day dogtrot cabin demonstrates a timelessness in aesthetic quality and physical endurance. The unhewn logs were undoubtedly carefully matched for size. Hewn heartwood piers—referred to in southern Georgia as pillars—provided support in the moist earth. The floors and purlins, door, and window frames are of sawn lumber, testifying to the many steam-operated sawmills in this timber region at the time the cabin was built. An interesting feature is that the cantilevers are round where they fit into the walls but gracefully hewn on the extensions, conferring a measure of delicacy on the entire building. A detached, two-room kitchen built of sawn lumber can be glimpsed at the rear.

Cantilever log at the Hooks Cabin. Its extensions, front and rear, are hewn to a square section.

Hand-hewn from the heart of a large longleaf pine, this pier is a typical feature of buildings in the southern coastal plain, where stones, which can be found only in riverbeds, are rarely used as a building material.

Below: Separate kitchens were the rule in southern Georgia as a precaution against fire. When the Clark Cabin was first built, cooking was done over the hearth in the house. Some years later the kitchen, which also had a stick-and-mud hearth and chimney, was constructed of sawn planks. The kitchen building consists of two rooms, one for cooking and the other for use as a dining room.

GEORGIA AGRIRAMA RESTORATION

near Tifton, Georgia

Log cabins on the south Georgia coastal plain in the late nineteenth century were built differently from cabins in the mountains during the same period. Reverend George Flournoy Clark constructed the story-and-a-half home above for his bride in 1885, near Tifton, Georgia. Seven of the twelve Clark children were born and reared here. The cabin has now been moved to the Georgia Agrirama Restoration near Tifton. The pine logs are relatively small in diameter and unhewn, although the bark has been removed. Corners are saddle-notched. Especially interesting is the stick-and-mud chimney, which was common in this area where stones were hard to come by, and the piers of hewn heart pine. Unlike the round sticks used for chimneys in the mountains, these chimney sticks were split from heart pine to dimensions of two inches by two inches. Heart pine, from the longleaf pine, was so impregnated with rosin that it was almost as rot-resistant as stone and was decidedly more rot-resistant than oak, chestnut, or locust. The cabin's roof extends to protect the mud chimney. Split boards were nailed over the cracks between the closely fitted logs instead of chinking.

The Preacher's House, built in the 1890s and partially restored at the Georgia Agrirama, shows another variation in log house construction. Round logs, saddle-notched at the corners, were used as a frame, which was weatherboarded with sawn vertical planks. Its distinction is that its extended corners project beyond the weatherboarding, clearly showing its origin as a log structure. It has a brick chimney.

Above: There was definite deterioration in the techniques used to construct log cabins between 1840 and 1890. The Clyatt House, built by a prosperous farmer around 1840, was originally situated in Tift County, Georgia. The building's square-notched corners and plumb lines, the small finely hewn logs, and the increased width of the cracks between the logs reflect the careful craftsmanship of the pre-Industrial Age; at that time, log cribs served as a kind of house frame. The Clyatt House is not weatherboarded, but the planed boards that cover the logs on the cabin's exterior blend so well with the hewn logs that one hardly notices this absence. The inside walls are sealed with sawn boards. The difference between the log buildings of 1840 and 1885 may well have been due to the difference in the sources of labor during the two periods. A prosperous farmer of 1840 in southern Georgia would surely have owned slaves. The dirt farmer of 1885 could rely on only his family and a few neighbors for help, leaving little time or money for refined craftsmanship.

Left: Painted board walls and nicely finished flooring made the Clyatt House as comfortable and elegant as most framed and weatherboarded houses of the 1840s. Quilt-making was an important domestic and social activity in the rural South until well into the twentieth century. Quilting frames were often suspended from the ceiling by ropes at each of their corners, so that the work could be raised out of the way of other activities during the day.

A watering trough hewn from a massive cypress log. Cypress logs of this size were rarely found after World War I. This trough, at the Georgia Agrirama near Tifton, Georgia, demonstrates the ingenuity and skill of American pioneers who relied on locally available resources for supplies and building materials.

The stick-and-mud chimney of the Clark cabin, with the characteristic extension of the roof to provide protection from rain. A firewood rack outside the window made the chore of refueling the fire easier.

HIGHWAY CABIN
North Carolina

Located on a highway in North Carolina a few miles north of Dillard, Georgia, this cabin is typical of the domiciles of Appalachia before roads were built in the area during the 1920s and 1930s. The cabin was unoccupied at the time this photograph was taken, but it apparently stands on its original site. While the shingle roof on the porch is still intact, the shingles of the crib have been covered by galvanized sheet roofing, a vulgarity that became quite common after the mountains were made accessible by highway. Highways allowed the log cabin dwellers to leave their rockbound farms and take jobs in factories where they made enough money to buy mass-produced metal roofing, which could be brought in on the highways.

CONLEY'S CREEK CABIN
Whittier, North Carolina

Above left: Located on Conley's Creek Road near Whittier, this deserted cabin has a rare mud-mortared stone chimney even though its roof has been modernized with tin. Its foundation is also mortared with mud and its chinking consists of stone and mud nogging.

Above right: An end view of the cabin with its rather narrow chimney and steep pitched roof. Despite the mud mortar in the chimney, the other details indicate that this dwelling was raised long after the region was settled, possibly in the early twentieth century. Log cabins were being built in this area as late as the 1920s, the construction methods unchanged since the eighteenth-century cabins, with only slight alterations in the design.

Left: Another unusual feature of the cabin is the arched fireplace opening. Like the chimney stones, these stones are bonded with mud, although a curved bar of iron supports the arch. In the center of the iron bar hangs a hook, undoubtedly used to hold cooking pots. Most cabins had hearths equipped either with cooking cranes or a bar in the back on which several S-shaped pothooks would hang.

QUALLA INDIAN RESERVATION
North Carolina

Built in 1840, shortly after the execution of the Cherokee hero Tsali Wasituna, the two-story cabin shown above served as a manse for the Cherokee United Methodist Church. The first minister of the church reared some twelve children here. The cabin, which was considered commodious for its day and its surroundings, originally stood a short distance from its present location, near the confluence of Wright's Creek and Soco Creek on the Qualla Indian Reservation. It was intermittently occupied by the minister of the church until the 1930s.

The typical Cherokee cabin pictured on the above right has been moved and authentically restored in the Soco Creek Valley on the Reservation. It is from the Big Cove area, the most isolated section of the reservation, which could be reached only by footpath until after World War II, when bulldozers and sophisticated technology forged new roads. The eastern Cherokees lived in this kind of cabin until well into the 1940s. There are still many Indians who know how to put up log cabins from sill to chimney.

Cherokee cabin builders persisted in making chimneys of sticks and mud even though stone was readily available in this area. At right, the chimney of the Big Cove cabin, which could have been found on numerous Indian cabins raised between the mid-eighteenth and the early twentieth centuries.

LOG TOWN HOUSES

Winston-Salem, North Carolina

A restored town house built of logs at Old Salem, a pre-revolutionary German settlement at Winston-Salem. The precise full-dovetail notching exhibits meticulous German workmanship. The delicate, rounded protrusions of the top wall logs, a feature absent from the frontier cabins of the nineteenth century, reflect the builder's taste for elegance.

Detail of the corner of the house. The end grain of the wall logs shows that they were hewn from the trunk rather than from split trees. The ends of the oak sill logs, which are rounded to match the top logs on all four walls, further the impression of elegance.

A smokehouse located behind one of the town houses. Its foundation is laid on a slope that has been dug out to provide storage space, accessible by a door in the rear. The building is similar to the cabins constructed by German settlers in Pennsylvania. The overhanging gable, which was typical of German design, was later adopted by settlers of Anglo-Saxon derivation in the early South. Of particular interest in the building is the cantilever, merely an extension of front and rear wall logs, which supports the shed on the right side.

A beautifully made log carriage house and servants' quarters behind another town house. Sill and top logs display the decorative finial found on many German buildings. The door is typical eighteenth-century batten construction. To the right is an ash hopper, which was used for making lye for soap, a necessity in the town and the woods.

PIONEER MUSEUM

Great Smoky Mountains National Park, North Carolina

A weary traveler coming over the mountain and viewing the Pioneer farm from a distance, the roofs of its outbuildings gleaming in the sun, livestock grazing in its fields, and men and women at work in the yard and shops, might feel hopeful of finding a haven for the night. Although typically American, this scene, lacking only a moat and watchtower, is reminiscent of the isolated, primitive baronies of Europe during the Dark Ages.

The apple house of the Pioneer farm exhibits possible German influence in its design. European barns often had a ground floor of stone with a log or board storage loft above.

Above: Each crib of this massive four-crib barn is carefully constructed of hewn logs fitted at the corners with half-dovetail notches. Like the roofs of most utilitarian buildings in the backwoods, the huge roof of this structure is covered with shakes, and the overhang provides ample room for storage of equipment and supplies. Ventilators in the gable end kept the hay stored in the loft from molding. The high doorway would have allowed a wagon laden with hay to be driven inside the building for unloading.

Left: The interior of the four-crib barn, with rafters and purlins. The hayrack on the end of one of the cribs could easily be filled from the hayloft. Cattle and horses would feed through the vertical sticks.

Above: A classic story-and-a-half Smoky Mountains farmhouse of pine logs, with an attached log kitchen. The glazed windows indicate the affluence of the family. Although this house and its outbuildings were moved from their original site to the Pioneer Museum in the Great Smoky Mountains National Park, North Carolina, at the time they were moved there were numerous craftsmen in the area who knew how to build with logs, how to split shingles, and how to construct chimneys of fieldstone. As a result, this restoration is more authentic than most. The horizontal boards in the gable are of a style that predated 1850. The bushes are boxwood. A chicken house, barn, and sorghum shed can be seen in the background.

Left: A front view of the farmhouse. Porches were often added as an afterthought to provide a place for sitting and for storage. In this house a round oak log on piers was used as a porch sill. Floor joists are mortised into the oak. The split shingle roof has a marvelous texture because some of the shingles curved slightly as they dried.

This view of the farmhouse reveals the careful notching of the logs on both house and kitchen. The chicken house stands behind the kitchen. None of the walls was chinked—the openings between logs were blocked by interior boards. The main section of the house is roofed with shingles whereas the more mundane kitchen and chicken house are covered with shakes, which, although easier to make, were less pretty.

This washing trough was hewn from a solid log of yellow poplar and was elevated to minimize bending. One basin is for washing, the other for rinsing. The trough is located on the bank of the Oconoluftee River at the Pioneer Museum farm in the Great Smoky Mountains National Park, North Carolina.

The massive storage barrel in this picture was made from a huge hollow gum tree and might have been used to store apples, cornmeal, or seeds.

Almost every backwoods homestead had a homemade shaving horse like this one, shown above left, which was fashioned from a fortuitously shaped tree. Shaving horses were treadle-operated clamps that held shingles, chair legs, or oxbows while the craftsman shaped or smoothed them with a drawknife or spokeshave.

Sleds were used for hauling year-round and were commonly found in the American backwoods from Maine to Florida. This sled, pictured at left, has runners of sourwood, which generally grew with a natural crook. Sourwood has a grain that will not splinter when pulled over earth or rocks.

In the photograph below, a group of bee gums. Bee gums made from hollow logs were a standard type of beehive used in pioneer America. Most backwoods farms had one or more of them on the place.

Hogs were valuable assets on mountain farms. Young pigs were secured
against the attack of bears in pens made of massive logs. The hog house
shown above, part of the Pioneer Museum farm at the Great Smoky
Mountains National Park in North Carolina, could withstand the attack
of the hungriest bruin.

Springhouses were built over or beside a small stream
so that the cool water could flow through an inside
trough in which milk and butter were refrigerated. This
view of the springhouse at the Pioneer Museum shows
a wooden pipe that was used to carry the flowing water
from the trough to the stream bed.

ANDREW JACKSON ESTATE
east of Nashville, Tennessee

Left: In 1804 Andrew Jackson, later to become the Hero of New Orleans in 1814 and President of the United States in 1828, bought the Hermitage Estate ten miles east of Nashville, Tennessee. At that time the only buildings on the estate's 425 acres were four log structures, of which only two have survived. These buildings were used as private dwellings and guesthouses until the brick mansion known as the Hermitage was completed in 1819. *Photograph by G. Holly*

Above right: Converted into a home by Andrew Jackson in 1804, the largest of the four log cabins on the estate was originally a blockhouse. This structure, which was initially intended to protect the early settlement from Cherokees, may have been raised as early as 1780, the date of the founding of the first settlement, which was to become Nashville. It's more likely, however, that the cabin was built either in 1785, when the Cherokees were finally defeated by the Tennessee militia, or in 1792, when the southern frontier was threatened by attacks from the fierce and undaunted Overhill Cherokees. Jackson, who was born in a log cabin on the South Carolina frontier before the American Revolution, must have felt at home in this house. *Photograph by G. Holly*

Right: The off-center front door is an unusual feature of Jackson's log house. This anomaly may be due to the cabin's originally having been a blockhouse. When the Jacksons lived here the building had two lean-tos at its back—one serving as a bedroom, the other as a pantry. The access to both lean-to rooms was probably from the outside only, since the building is without a back door. Jackson had the distinction of being the first United States president born in a log cabin. A number of his successors to the office won by appealing to the growing frontier electorate through an association, sometimes quite remote, with the log cabin, symbol of the American backwoods. *Photograph by G. Holly*

Right: Many prominent people visited Andrew Jackson and were lodged in the humble log structures he used as his guesthouses. President James Monroe, when he made the first visit to Tennessee of any incumbent chief executive, and Aaron Burr, during his visit to the Hermitage in 1805 and 1806, were both recipients of Jackson's hospitality. Jefferson Davis, later to become Secretary of War and President of the Confederate States of America, stayed in one of these houses as a boy, in 1815. According to Davis, "General Jackson's house at that time was a roomy log house. In front of it was a grove of fine forest trees, and behind it were his cotton and grain fields." *Photograph by G. Holly*

Below right: This beautifully made hand-wrought strap hinge is on Andrew Jackson's house. The present shutter seems to be a replacement, and the new boards clearly did not fit the nail holes punched for the original shutter. *Photograph by G. Holly*

Left: Of the three guesthouses at the original Hermitage, only one remains, and information about the other two is scant. President Polk's wife recalled that near the blockhouse "were three smaller houses, one story high, with low attics." The survivor is an excellent example of a double-pen house. The pens are separated by a wall of interior logs, with a massive chimney of Tennessee limestone at each end. The roof is at a low angle, as were the roofs of most log cabins before 1850. *Photograph by G. Holly*

PETER CABLE PLACE

Cades Cove, Tennessee

Above left: This view of the Peter Cable barn in Cades Cove reveals the opening in the barn's half-walls. A common feature in barns at this time, the opening enabled a wagon laden with hay to be driven between the cribs for convenient unloading in the hayloft.

Above right: A fine smokehouse at the Cable place. The Cable family, which owned a mill and blacksmith shop as well as a sawmill, lived in a frame house covered with clapboards, but most of the utilitarian buildings here were of logs. This smokehouse, or meat house, was used for storing country-cured ham and bacon. The removable floorboards were hewn and adzed to a silky smoothness. The overhanging gable indicates German influence.

Left: These rafters are typical of log buildings before about 1870. They are made of peeled saplings, mitered together without a ridgepole. Purlins, split or rough sawn, support the roofing. This is an interior view of the Cable's cantilevered barn.

Shown opposite, the log piers supporting the millrace at Cable's grist mill in Cades Cove.

The backwoods ash hopper pictured at top is typical of its kind. Fireplace ashes were put into the hopper, and water was allowed to filter through. The resulting lye was necessary for making soap. When lye was being made, the hopper was placed over a large cast-iron washpot or barrel.

The door of the Cable meat house, shown above, is entirely without metal. Even when nails were readily available and hinges could be made in the blacksmith shop, many mountain craftsmen continued to rely on the old materials.

Facing page: A cabin on the Peter Cable place in which one end, the side toward the prevailing wind, is weatherboarded. Weatherboarding reinforced the mud chinking and made the building much warmer when the winter winds blew.

Below: Log construction for utility buildings as well as dwellings continued to be used in the South until World War I. An unusual design, this half log, half board two-crib barn is behind the Cable House on the Peter Cable place in Cades Cove, Tennessee.

Above: Blacksmith shops in the backwoods were frequently constructed of roughly hewn, saddle-notched logs. These buildings were usually unchinked and often had shake roofs. The shops were equipped with an anvil mounted on a log butt, bellows, and a forge made of either fieldstone or saplings and lined with mud and fieldstones. Most blacksmith shops did not bother with the luxury of a flue: the smoke would rise out through cracks between the shakes on the roof. This shop is at Cable's mill on the Peter Cable place in Cades Cove, Tennessee.

Left: The gate at Cable's store, built of split and roughly pointed palings of white oak. Its form is reminiscent of the typical English hurdle gate.

MONTGOMERY-TARWATER CABIN
Greenback, Tennessee

Built by Mr. Montgomery for his bride in 1846, this cabin, on its original site near Greenback, is lovingly maintained by its present occupants, the Tarwater family. The structure is of story-and-a-half design; a narrow staircase in one corner of the ground floor provides access to the upper floor. Although the additions are modern, the shingle walls of the new part, with weathering, will eventually come to match the venerable logs of the original cabin. Some of the windows in the log building were probably added years after the house was raised.

An interior view of the Montgomery-Tarwater Cabin. The original fireplace and chimney are made of brick. The typical high, narrow stairway in the background leads to the second story. Both brickwork and stairs give this cabin a more sophisticated appearance than its backwoods counterparts. In most backwoods cabins, fireplaces and hearths were generally of fieldstone, and ladders or pegs driven into wall logs took the place of stairs.

JOHN OLIVER CABIN
Cades Cove, Tennessee

The John Oliver Cabin in Cades Cove, Tennessee, is now included in the Great Smoky Mountains National Park. Although Oliver was the first settler of this beautiful, isolated valley, he did not build this cabin until the 1850s. Of story-and-a-half design, the structure has the unusual distinction of having porches in both front and back. The yard is surrounded by a worm fence of split rails, which served to keep cattle and horses out of the garden.

A closer view of the cabin. The chimney is built of fieldstone mortared with cement, a material available in the Cove by the 1850s. Both cabin and chimney are solidly constructed. The porches, on the other hand, seem downright rickety, yet they have stood for one hundred and twenty years. The cabin is located quite close to a spring and is supported on fieldstone piers. A root cellar was not necessary when a springhouse could be built close by.

A fine cantilever barn on the Oliver place. This barn, which has been moved to its present site, is typical of the sturdy outbuildings found around pioneer homesteads. Of double-crib construction, the Cades Cove barn lacks the majestic size and elaborately constructed roof of the four-crib barn at the Pioneer farm in the Great Smoky Mountains National Park. (See p. 123.) Yet its precise workmanship and fine, natural proportions make this building a classic. The cantilevers are hewn on a taper to the outside ends, intended both to save weight and to lessen the strain on the supporting center. The taper lends a natural grace to the huge timbers and to the structure as a whole. Cantilever barns are an expression of the German influence on log buildings of this period.

An ingenious gate in the worm fence surrounding the John Oliver Cabin in Cades Cove, Tennessee. The **V**-shaped design provided access to both people and dogs while keeping cattle and horses from entering the garden inside the fence.

The John Oliver family obviously included a cat or two. This interior shot shows a cat hole neatly sawn in the bottom of one of the doors. There's an old story about a man who had three cats and three holes in his door. When asked why, he said, "When I say scat, I mean *scat!*"

BROTHERTON CABIN
Chattanooga, Tennessee

This antebellum cabin stands on its original site not far from the Kelly Cabin at Chickamauga and Chattanooga National Military Park (see p. 111), near Chattanooga, Tennessee. At first glance, except for its restored chimney, the Brotherton Cabin seems almost identical with the Kelly Cabin. However, there are distinct differences in the design of these two buildings, and some of them are wholly cultural. In accordance with English tradition and the English derivation of the family name, the Brotherton Cabin is more square in its dimensions than the Kelly Cabin. Also, whereas the logs of the Scotch-Irish Kelly structure are joined by typical saddle notching, the notches on this cabin are half-dovetail.

Even though the chimney of the Brotherton Cabin is of cement-mortared stone, the extending roof suggests that the mortar used originally was mud. The cabin is entirely without windows and is a story and a half in height. The ceiling on the ground-floor level is quite low, barely six feet. The two doors are just five feet high, requiring even a short person to stoop when entering. Top logs are cantilevered on one end to provide support for the extended roof on the chimney end.

An interesting feature of the Brotherton Cabin, which is otherwise typical in its design and construction, is that on the end opposite the chimney the top log projects about a foot. This detail is reminiscent of German cabin construction. Unlike the beautifully crafted log buildings at the Moravian settlement of Old Salem, however, the end is square, undecorated, and as utilitarian as the other features of this structure. Yet it does add a bit of distinction.

KENTUCKY CABINS
In downtown Shelbyville, Kentucky, the cabin at left was discovered hiding beneath clapboarding only when the building was being razed. According to local tales it was once a stagecoach stop. The second story is reached by a narrow enclosed stairway. This cabin was probably intended to be weatherboarded originally rather than left with exposed logs.

Nice proportions and an impressive chimney are the outstanding features of this cabin located near Louisville, Kentucky. Limestone is common to this region, and it is most suitable for chimney bases. Most early chimneys in Kentucky had a limestone base and a cats-and-clay flue, but brick or cut limestone eventually became the flue material for later chimneys.

Built near Bardstown, Kentucky, around 1804, this attractive one-room structure was eventually moved to Shelbyville, where it was restored and currently serves as a private museum of the early days of Kentucky. Most of the log cabins in Kentucky, at least those that have survived, seem to have been one-crib, story-and-a-half structures, making this cabin at Shelbyville unusual.

The dogtrot cabin pictured at left was restored and made into a lovely home near Louisville. It was originally built about 1810 on the General (later to become President) Zachary Taylor tract and then moved to the grounds of Farmington Mansion. Its dogtrot has been enclosed to provide a central interior hall, an improvement often made as cabins evolved into houses. It is used today as a private home.

A fine example of a story-and-a-half dogtrot cabin on the grounds of Locust Grove Mansion near Louisville, Kentucky. The state was blessed in its early days with a variety of trees that could be used for building cabins. These included poplar, oak, chestnut, ash, cedar, locust, and pine. Wall logs would sometimes be of elegant and durable walnut, floors were made of oak and ash, and interior trim was often of walnut or cherry.

An original privy with traditional door decorations behind a restored log cabin in Kentucky, near Louisville. Many backwoods cabins set in the privacy of the wilderness dispensed with such amenities. As settlements grew, however, privies became necessary. By that time sawmills would have been set up, making sawn lumber available.

1810 HOUSE

Washington County, Louisiana

Above: This log house, built about 1810, is somewhat unusual. It is constructed of pine logs that have been hewn into boards about three inches thick and given square notches for the corners. As a result, the interstices between the logs are minimal. The sills extend out to support the end porch, which is another unusual feature. The porch door and the front door give access to the one room. The cabin has the rather rare distinction of having once been whitewashed.

Left: The hearth of the 1810 House. From the side wall it's possible to see how thin the clay wall of the hearth was. Apparently the hearth floor was made of packed clay and rested on the ground two or more feet below. If allowed to thoroughly dry before a fire was built, a hearth and chimney of this sort could be burned into one solid, functionally shaped brick. This porcelain fireplace was the counterpart of the porcelain stoves widespread in northern Europe during the eighteenth and nineteenth centuries. The cabin's roof has been extended to protect the clay chimney from rain.

Below: The chimney of the 1810 House in Washington County, Louisiana, is made of sticks and clay, no doubt because stone was hard to come by in this area. The piers supporting the house, however, are of stone. The gable ends are of hewn logs instead of boards, which was common for the period before 1840. The bottom wall log in front seems to have been sawn with a circular saw rather than hewn. Since circular saws were not in use until the 1850s, one may presume that this particular timber is a replacement.

Above: This interesting corncrib is one of the outbuildings of the 1810 House. It's difficult to ascertain its date from construction details. For instance, the ridgepole was not common in most areas until the 1870s, yet rafters lap-jointed in the mode of the 1830s or earlier are resting on the ridgepole instead of being fastened to it in the style of the 1870s. Also, the building is constructed of logs from trees that were felled by ax instead of the crosscut saw relied on in the 1870s. The logs in the lower courses are heavier than those above, a scheme that conserved a great deal of energy when hoisting the upper logs into position.

LOWER AND UPPER SWEDISH CABINS
Upper Darby Creek, Pennsylvania

Known as the Lower Swedish Cabin, this cabin was built by Swedish settlers on Upper Darby Creek near Philadelphia around 1650. It was occupied continuously for three hundred years. It will be restored by the state of Pennsylvania, although, despite its age, the structure will actually require only minimal restoration. Made of round, unbarked logs of several species of trees, **V**-notched at the corner, this cabin is the prototypical pioneer dwelling brought from Scandinavia to become an integral part of life in the New World.

The original cabin had only one room. Shortly after it was built, however, another crib was attached.

The joining of the two cribs of the Lower Swedish Cabin on Upper Darby Creek, Pennsylvania, is unusual in that the logs of the second room are butted into the end wall of the first and held in position by two hewn vertical boards, which are pegged to the slightly hewn log ends and the corner of the first room. This method of joining is similar to French construction of log cabins. Chinking for this cabin is mud and stone nogging.

Rough, unbarked poles, pegged at the apex, form the rafters of the Lower Swedish Cabin. This sort of joining continued to be used for rafters in log cabins until the 1870s.

This fireplace in one of the rooms of the Lower Swedish Cabin has a lintel of stones that were probably found in nearby Upper Darby Creek.

Above: Also on Upper Darby Creek near Philadelphia stands another Swedish log cabin built ca. 1650 and known as the Upper Swedish Cabin. In plan and construction, it mirrors the Lower Swedish Cabin, even in the use of V-notched unbarked logs for building material. Unfortunately the interior of this cabin has been radically changed over the centuries. For instance, there were probably one or two corner fireplaces in the original structure, but they have since been replaced by modern wood stoves. This cabin has a stone foundation and a roomy cellar, which is its main distinction from the Lower Cabin.

Left: Although almost identical with the corner fireplace in the other room, this fireplace in the Lower Swedish Cabin on Upper Darby Creek in Pennsylvania, is without a stone lintel. Built completely within the log walls, the fireplace resembles an immovable stone stove. As was common in early fireplaces, the hearth lintel here is a large hewn timber. Somewhat charred on its interior, the lintel served all this cabin's inhabitants from about 1650 until 1965.

JOHN MORTON HOMESTEAD
Prospect Park, Pennsylvania

The John Morton Homestead in Prospect Park, Pennsylvania, close to Philadelphia. Its first room, on the right, was built on this site in 1654 by Morton Mortonson, a Swedish settler, on Darby Creek in what was then a part of New Sweden. Later, in 1689, an adjacent cabin was built, creating a dogtrot plan. Sometime in the eighteenth century the dogtrot was enclosed by stone walls, and the loft was made into sleeping quarters in 1835 when the building was used as a tavern. Occupied continuously from 1654 to 1936, this fine house was the birthplace of John Morton, a signer of the Declaration of Independence and a great-grandson of the builder.

Left: Built of large hewn logs of mixed species, the building exhibits fine craftsmanship in the half-dovetail notches of its corners. In the end facing Darby Creek, which was navigable in 1654, is what is presumed to be a musket port, a long slit that could be covered by a board on the inside. Muskets would not have been needed against the friendly Lenni Lenape Indians in the area but might have proved useful when hostile Dutch intruders conquered New Sweden about the time this cabin was built.

Above: The musket port as seen from the inside. It was covered by a board resting in two wooden brackets when not in use.

Both of the lower rooms of the Morton House were used for sleeping, sitting, and cooking. This bed is typical of the furniture that might have been found in the house in the eighteenth century. The interior walls of the room were at one time whitewashed to increase the light from the small windows.

Left: In 1835 when a loft was finished for sleeping quarters in the Morton House in Prospect Park, Pennsylvania, it was accessible by this and one other narrow stairway.

Below: Unlike most later dogtrot cabins, the chimneys in the Morton Homestead were built next to the dogtrot. The huge walk-in hearths, with massive hewn wooden lintels, were built of stone and furnished with cranes for cooking.

SWEDISH GRANARY
Greenwich, New Jersey

The only surviving Swedish log granary in America. Following traditional Swedish design, this building is divided inside by a log wall to create a threshing floor and a storage bin. Built ca. 1650, the granary has been moved two miles from its original site on the Elmer Gandy farm and restored behind the historical museum in Greenwich, New Jersey. This area, close to the mouth of the Delaware River, was part of New Sweden, a colony founded in 1638, whose settlers originally brought the concept of log buildings to America.

This rear view of the Swedish granary shows the ends of the logs that formed the interior wall and the floor joists of the loft. Also shown is the typical early Swedish roof made of long boards, which overlapped like shingles with a layer of bark in between.

Far left: An inside shot of the Swedish granary in Greenwich, New Jersey, showing the log interior wall and a log ladder leading to the loft. American log form structures were usually divided inside by plank walls. An exception, perhaps a relic of Swedish influence, is the barn at the Tullie Smith House Restoration in Atlanta (see p. 101).

Left: As was the custom in seventeenth-century Sweden, the loft of this granary was used as a girls' dormitory during the summer. Rough plank beds were filled with hay or straw left from the threshing, which served as a fresh and easily renewable mattress.

Below, far left: Wrought-iron hinges on the door of the granary very much resemble American wrought-iron barn hinges.

Below left: The long boards overlapping on the granary roof were presumably split and then laid with bark between the two layers.

HYDE CABIN

Grand Isle, Vermont

The home of Jedediah Hyde, Jr., and his descendants in Grand Isle, Vermont, for about one hundred fifty years, this log cabin, which Hyde erected in 1783, has some interesting features. The structure is divided into two rooms within a single pen by a central hallway, unlike the dogtrot cabins of the South. Before being moved a couple of miles from its original site and restored in 1956, the cabin had two brick chimneys, which may or may not have been part of the initial construction. The near chimney in this photograph, however, shows no hearth-back outside the walls, suggesting that either it replaced a French Canadian or Swedish-type interior hearth or that it is a more contemporary modification built for the installation of a stove. Cabins divided by a hallway usually had a fireplace at each end. Log buildings were rare in New England. *Photograph courtesy of Vermont Division for Historic Preservation*

After restoration, with some of its original timbers replaced, the Hyde Cabin took on a slightly different appearance. Vertical boards now enclosed the gables, and one of the chimneys has disappeared. The small closed-in opening beside a front window indicates that the glazed windows were put in some time after the cabin was raised. Although it is "considered the oldest log cabin in the United States still standing in its original condition," this description does not take into account the three Swedish colonial cabins of 1650 vintage that remain, two of them unrestored, near Philadelphia. *Photograph courtesy of Vermont Division for Historic Preservation*

SARIBAULT CABIN
Minnesota

The French settlers of Canada and the old Northwest used a different technique for building log structures. The Saribault Cabin, now restored at Murphy's Landing State Park outside of Minneapolis, Minnesota, was originally built in 1844 at Shakopee Springs, only a few miles from where it has since been moved and restored. Vertical channeled posts are located in the center of each wall, and the hearth and chimney are completely within the walls, similar to the corner fireplaces of early Swedish cabins. ***Photo courtesy Jim Mone***

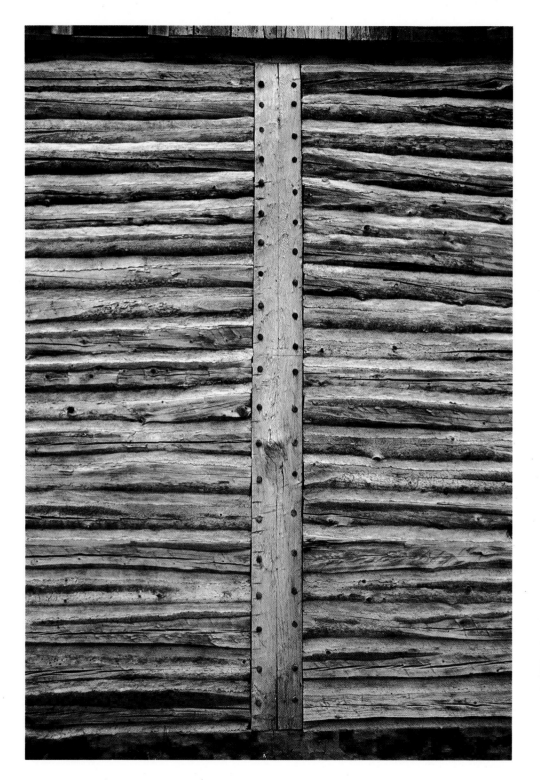

Left: The vertical channeled posts in the center of each wall are peculiar to French-American cabins. The center end of every wall log was hewn to fit into the channel, which was about three inches deep. The log was then securely pegged into position. This method allowed for the construction of a more commodious cabin with short logs from small trees of the types often found in northwesterly latitudes. *Photo courtesy Jim Mone*

Below: Almost as unusual as the use of posts is the flat notching of the Saribault Cabin. Wall logs, dressed with minimal hewing, are joined at the notches in pairs and sometimes shimmed with cleft boards to achieve a horizontal plane for some of the logs. Corners built in this way lack the interlocking strength provided by dovetail, half-dovetail, or saddle notching. The courses of logs may be pegged together at the corners, but it's impossible to prove this point without partially dismantling the building. *Photo courtesy Jim Mone*

JOE CARR HOUSE
Tacoma, Washington

Although the Joe Carr House in the Old Town section of Tacoma, Washington, is described as the oldest residence in the community, one wonders how well it could have served as a home since it has no chimneys. In 1864 when it was built, however, it might have been heated by a cast-iron stove brought by ship " 'round the Horn." The two windows in the front wall would indicate that the early Washington state settlers felt more secure about Indians than the earlier settlers of the East. The eastern cabins often had no windows at all, or at best a single small window next to the chimney. This building was also the first post office in the Tacoma area. *Photograph by Capt. John O. Ellis, Jr., USA*

The Carr House is a curious mixture of old and new design. Apparently heated by a stove, which was certainly modern in 1864, the building retains the low-angled roof, and log purlins and shake, rather than shingle, roofing, which was rare in the East after 1820. Its unhewn logs follow a much earlier tradition, reminiscent of the Swedish cabins in Pennsylvania of the mid-seventeenth century. This structure resembles the cabins built along the Missouri River during the 1870s, which were also heated by stoves. Nevertheless, the basic log construction of the Carr House served its purpose in providing quickly built shelter against a hostile environment, once again illustrating the practicality of the log cabin as a major factor in settling America. *Photograph by Capt. John O. Ellis, Jr., USA*

FORT NISQUALLY
Tacoma, Washington

Fort Nisqually on Puget Sound outside of Tacoma, Washington, was founded by the Hudson Bay Company in 1833, when the ownership and use of the Oregon Territory was in dispute between the United States and Canada. The design of its blockhouses, one of which is shown here, reflects a kinship with both the American/English forts in the East during the eighteenth century and the seventeenth-century Swedish log fort at the Skansen Museum in Stockholm. The construction, however, follows the model of French Canadian log structures, with horizontal logs mortised into channels in upright corner posts and pegged securely into place. *Photograph courtesy Old Fort Nisqually*

Built in 1843, some twenty years earlier than the Joe Carr House in Tacoma, the granary at Fort Nisqually on Puget Sound, outside of Tacoma, is the oldest standing structure in the state of Washington. Part of the original Hudson's Bay Company complex, this utility building was raised by British, Scottish, and Orkney Islander laborers indentured to the Hudson's Bay Company for five years. Apparently the expedition included French Canadians, too, and since the indentured laborers had had no exposure to log construction, it may be safely assumed that French Canadians designed the log buildings that the laborers assembled. Ironically, the Orkney Islands were originally settled in the ninth century by Vikings who did have a tradition of log buildings. However, since the Islands had no appreciable supply of timber, doubtless the methods of building with logs had been forgotten by Orkney people long before 1843. *Photograph by Capt. John O. Ellis, Jr., USA*

orkney is in Puget sound [story]

Like other log buildings at Fort Nisqually, the store building displays typical French Canadian style construction. All the log buildings at this fort are distinguished by the way their vertical channel posts are mortised and pegged into the sills instead of being sunk in the ground. *Photograph by Capt. John O. Ellis, Jr., USA*

Fort Nisqually's blacksmith shop was built between 1833 and 1843 and reconstructed in 1934 with some of its original timber and some replacement timber. All log buildings at Fort Nisqually were built before 1854 when a sawmill was established at the post. *Photograph by Capt. John. O. Ellis, Jr., USA*

Also of logs, although its later additions were covered by split shingles, the Chief Trader's House was reconstructed in 1934. Most of the personnel at this Hudson's Bay Company post married Indian women and lived with their families outside the stockade. This might explain the absence of chimneys in a building called a house. An artist's reconstruction of the original post, however, depicts this structure with chimneys. It is likely that typical French Canadian fireplaces were originally built entirely within the log walls of this house. These could well have deteriorated by 1934 and consequently been overlooked in the reconstruction of that time. *Photograph by Capt. John O. Ellis, Jr., USA*

FORT ROSS

north of San Francisco, California

Above: Fort Ross, which has been restored north of San Francisco, California, shows yet another influence in American log structures in addition to the Swedish and Scotch-Irish, English, German, and French Canadian styles. Fort Ross was established by Russians in 1812, to protect their valuable sea otter hunting grounds from Spanish traders who were moving north along the California coast. Its restored buildings are of massive and enduring redwood logs, hewn to precise dimensions. Located near Sutter's Mill, Fort Ross was abandoned about the time of the California Gold Rush and incorporated in the Sutter holdings. It was later sold and became part of a cattle ranch. *Photograph by Gene R. Russell*

Left: Russians undoubtedly learned the methods of log construction from Swedish Vikings who penetrated the forests the Slav inhabited on the northern end of Europe before the year 1000. The octagonal tower at one angle of the stockade at Fort Ross reflects an affinity to Swedish building styles—its form is almost identical with the octagonal windmills used in Sweden from the eleventh to the nineteenth century.

Photograph by Gene R. Russell

ST. MARY'S MISSION
Stevensville, Montana

This mission, located in the heart of the Old West, was founded in 1841 by Father Pierre Jean de Smet, a Belgian Jesuit, and built by Father Antonio Ravalli. Both men were well-known missionaries who tended to the spiritual needs of Indians and settlers alike. The mission, still in excellent condition, is constructed of cottonwood logs. *Photograph courtesy Ronald Woodall*

MINER'S CABIN
Cody, Wyoming

Built originally in 1890 at Greybull River, Wyoming, and now restored in Cody, Wyoming, this miner's cabin, with beautifully hewn and notched logs, is much more elegant than the temporary cabins hastily thrown together by most of the gold miners. At this late date, perhaps the man who built it realized the impossibility of getting rich overnight and planned to stay in this cabin for several years. The low roof and the quality of the craftsmanship suggest that the builder was a Scandinavian immigrant skilled in the use of an ax. *Photograph courtesy Ronald Woodall*

TEDDY ROOSEVELT RANCH HOUSE
Medora, North Dakota

This log house, formerly located on the Maltese Cross Ranch near Medora, North Dakota, was once the home of Teddy Roosevelt. After his wife and his mother died within a few months of each other in 1884, Roosevelt, who had spent a vacation hunting buffalo in North Dakota the previous year, decided to establish a ranch in the state. Roosevelt lived in this house on the Maltese Cross Ranch for about a year and a half beginning in 1884 and then moved to a house on the Elkhorn Ranch a few miles north. That house, which Roosevelt maintained until 1888 or 1889, does not survive today. The Maltese Cross house was moved from its original site to be displayed at the 1904 World's Fair in St. Louis and is presently situated at the Theodore Roosevelt Memorial Park in Medora. ***Photograph courtesy Ronald Woodall***

"ROBBER'S ROOST"
Sheridan, Montana

Picturesquely dubbed the "Robber's Roost," this tavern was built by Peter Daly in 1863. It was a popular hangout for highwaymen of the Old West in the days before law enforcement was a reality. Except for the lack of a massive stone chimney, this building closely resembles taverns built earlier in the East, such as Vann's Tavern in Georgia (p. 84) and the Crockett Tavern in Tennessee (p. 11). ***Photograph courtesy Ronald Woodall***

Canada

In Canada, the tradition of log cabins runs as strong and deep as in the United States. In fact, Canadian log structures, perhaps more varied in style and history, are very likely of earlier origins than their counterparts in the United States. It is distinctly possible that in 1602, five years before the founding of Virginia and a generation before New Sweden, the first French settlement of New Brunswick was composed of log buildings that were prototypes of the buildings put up by later French Canadians. Some of the early French settlers in Canada were from the coast of Normandy and had probably inherited their knowledge of building with logs from the Norse who founded that area.

The French method of building, known as *pièces-sur-pièces*, was best suited to the small trees that grew in eastern Canada. *Pièces-sur-pièces* construction consists of tenoning vertical posts into horizontal sills and fitting tenoned logs into channels in the posts, as illustrated on page 45. The same method, which some authorities believe to have orginated in the *bulhuse* construction of ancient Denmark, can also be seen in many log buildings in modern Scandinavia. On this continent, *pièces-sur-pièces* construction was later adopted by the British who settled in Canada after the French. Although there are some examples of this construction technique in Minnesota and Oregon, it is decidedly Canadian, of French derivation.

But the most interesting facet of the story of Canadian log cabins is the variety of cultures that their tradition reflects. In the late nineteenth century, immigrants from northern Europe contributed a wide range of styles of log construction to the westward-moving frontier. The English, Welsh, Scots, and Irish, who came in great numbers were exposed to log buildings only after their arrival in Canada. However, the Norwegians, Swedes, Finns, Russians, and Germans were already familiar with log buildings and the techniques for putting them together. And in the late nineteenth century Americans experienced in log construction, like Sam McGee of Tennessee, were drawn into the gold fields of the Yukon, where log cabins and barns were found in abundance.

Quite a few relics remain of the log structures that these various groups built; they are still used as homes and utility buildings in the wilderness of Manitoba, Alberta, Saskatchewan, British Columbia, and the Yukon. There are elegant log structures, raised by Ukrainian pioneers,

MINER'S CABIN
Dawson City, Yukon
Unhewn logs, single saddle notching, and the general proportions of this cabin at Dawson City, Yukon, point to its probable origin as a miner's cabin built hastily during the Klondike gold rush of 1899. The off-center door and large glazed window reflect later design influences rather than those of the early frontier. *Photograph courtesy Ronald Woodall*

to be found in Saskatchewan, with their round logs saddle-notched in the Russian manner and plastered thickly with mud that was then white-washed, and their hip roofs covered with thatch. In old photographs from areas of British Columbia that were settled by Scandinavians in the late nineteenth century one can find log buildings displaying the typical proportions of ancient log structures from Sweden or Norway, their low roofs covered with birchbark and sod or split boards. In the Yukon there are cabins built by Americans that are reminiscent of the dwellings of Appalachia, but these usually have round logs rather than the hewn logs of the American structures.

The log cabin tradition has been more continuous in Canada than in the United States. From 1886 on, when the Canadian Pacific Railroad completed its transcontinental line, putting in spurs to isolated farming and timber country north and south of the main line, logs were available in abundance in any part of Canada. Pioneers of that era still cut cabin logs with ax and crosscut saw, and dragged them to the building site by horse or ox. Later, as the country across Canada was settled and new passenger stops established, the railroad began to build many of its stations with logs that were often shipped from the rain forests of the British Columbian coast. And still later, in 1930, when Canadian Pacific built the largest log structure in the world, the thousands of logs needed were shipped by train from the west coast. Originally a lodge, this building was eventually converted into a hotel, Le Chateau Montebello, with one hundred eighty-six rooms and a lobby one hundred feet in diameter. The plans and construction of the train stations and Le Chateau Montebello alike were created and supervised by architects, a modern practice that would have been scorned by the *coureurs du bois* of olden Canada, but which gave new impetus to log buildings in the modern nation.

Enthusiasm for building new log houses seems to be waxing stronger and stronger in the Canada of the 1970s. In fact, Canada has the world's only magazine devoted to log building, *The Canadian Log House,* published once a year in the spring. In addition to building new log houses of contemporary style for contemporary living, Canada continues to lavish great care on restoring old forts and fur posts comprised of log buildings. And since Canada can claim many different cultural styles for its log buildings, it is probably the showcase of the world for variety, comfort, beauty, and ingenuity of houses made of logs, from both the past and the present.

Above: The attractive Canadian Pacific Railway station in Montebello, Quebec, is impressive in size and physical detail. Although built in 1930 and based on an architect's design, the building's construction out of logs brought by rail from distant British Columbia ties it in to early Canadian history. With its two massive stone chimneys, which give it the appearance of a grand hunting lodge, the station at Montebello serves as an architectural link between Canada's past and present. *Photograph courtesy Canadian Pacific Railway*

Left: Constructed in the late 1880s, these buildings of the Canadian Pacific Railway station in Banff, Alberta, are graceful in their use of details such as hip roofs and multisash windows. This photograph was taken in 1888, two years after the transcontinental line was completed. *Photograph courtesy Canadian Pacific Railway*

Below left: This finely constructed log station at High Falls, Ontario, evokes the aura of the Canadian frontier. Raised in about 1886 by the Kingston and Pembroke Railway, which was later absorbed by the Canadian Pacific, the High Falls station is an example of outstanding craftsmanship in log construction. Of particular interest are the building's finely hewn logs, its precise half-dovetail corner notches, and its roof, which was made of whole logs shaped by the foot adz to fit together like Mediterranean tile. The structure's roof and proportions suggest that its design is of Scandinavian origin. Since many Norwegian and Swedish immigrants worked on railroad construction during this period, it is in fact likely that the station was put up by Scandinavians, most of whom were natural craftsmen. *Photograph courtesy Canadian Pacific Railway*

SAM McGEE CABIN

Whitehorse, Yukon

Sam McGee from Tennessee, the protagonist of Robert Service's beloved poem, "The Cremation of Sam McGee," raised this cabin in 1899 when he trekked to Whitehorse, Yukon, to hunt for gold. With its unhewn logs and saddle-notched corners, the cabin would easily fit into any valley of the Tennessee mountains settled by a Scotch-Irish family. *Photograph courtesy National Film Board of Canada Photothèque/Photo by Crombie McNeill, 1976*

ROBERT SERVICE CABIN

Dawson City, Yukon

Mr. Service could easily have gathered the grist for his poetry mill from his small log cabin at Dawson City, Yukon. Log buildings, even though roughly built, could be erected quickly to provide comfortable shelter against the subarctic winter. According to Service's poem, Sam McGee froze to death and was revived only after he had been enclosed in a crematorium for several hours. *Photograph courtesy National Film Board of Canada Photothèque/Photo by Crombie McNeill, 1976*

MOUNT ROBSON CABINS

British Columbia

Pictured here at the foot of Mount Robson are log buildings of the modern frontier in British Columbia. These structures, dating from well into the twentieth century, combine the logs of the native British Columbian forests with the modern feature of tar-paper roofs. After 1886, the railroad made tar paper available to a large part of the Canadian frontier. Despite the modern roofing, these buildings meld naturally with the surrounding wilderness. ***Photograph courtesy National Film Board of Canada Photothèque/Photo by E. Bork, 1962***

MAGOG LAKE CABIN

British Columbia

A modern log cabin that serves as a camp at Magog Lake, British Columbia. Mount Assiniboine may be seen in the background. The building almost seems to be growing on its site like the trees from which it is made. Logs are the perfect building material for such isolated spots, and they offer far more durability and warmth than other construction staples. ***Photograph courtesy National Film Board of Canada Photothèque/Photo by George Hunter, 1973***

COTTONWOOD HOUSE

British Columbia

Located on the Cariboo Road, this roadhouse (which contains a stable and a barn as well) was built by the Boyd family in 1864 during the height of the Cariboo gold rush. The house is an elaborate and rather unusual log structure. Hewn logs and half-dovetail notches follow the American tradition, but the log wing and shed are more Swedish in origin. The general house plan is in keeping with the design of most frame houses of the period. ***Photograph courtesy Ronald Woodall***

Detail of the exterior of this beautiful house, overgrown with greenery. *Photograph courtesy Ronald Woodall*

The barn of the Cottonwood House. *Photograph courtesy Ronald Woodall*

FORT SAINT JAMES

British Columbia

Built in 1888 by the Hudson Bay Company, this fort, of *pièces-sur-pièces* construction, is located far north of Vancouver. The large hip-roofed building pictured was probably used as a store or warehouse. It exemplifies French-Canadian log construction, as does Fort Nisqually in the state of Washington (pp. 161- 63), even though the latter was built some thirty years earlier by the Hudson Bay Company. *Photograph courtesy Ronald Woodall*

LOG CHURCH

Ashcroft, British Columbia

This log church, located near Ashcroft, British Columbia, is part of a group of log buildings that make up the Cornwall Indian Reserve. The church is known, interestingly enough, as the Church of St. John at the Latin Gate. It was built in 1891 by the Cornwall brothers, one of whom became lieutenant governor of British Columbia. *Photograph courtesy Ronald Woodall*

LOG HOUSE
Didsbury, Saskatchewan

Residual furring strips on the sides of this handsome building in Didsbury, Saskatchewan, indicate that it was originally intended to be a log house frame, covered with weatherboarding in the manner of houses built in the late eighteenth century in the United States. The origin of the builders is unknown, but the proportions of the house strongly resemble Swedish manor houses of the seventeenth century. The inside fireplace (as shown by the location of the chimney) also points to the probable Swedish design influence. *Photograph courtesy Ronald Woodall*

UKRAINIAN FARMHOUSE
Caliento, Manitoba

Built in 1911, this beautiful Ukrainian farmhouse was lived in until 1967. Constructed of stucco over logs, it has a picturesque (and rare, in North America) thatched roof. Although the house was built long after the railroads made modern building materials available in much of Manitoba, it could fit easily into a Russian or Scandinavian farm village of the middle ages. The central chimney probably indicates an enclosed fireplace similar to those found in Scandinavian and French-Canadian log houses. *Photograph courtesy Ronald Woodall*

GHOST TOWN

Quesnel Forks, British Columbia

This rather mysterious-looking ghost town in western Canada has been abandoned since 1920. The buildings were built in 1861 by the Royal Engineers as a supply center during the gold rush.

Pictured above, is a rather ramshackle, but utterly charming, building in Quesnel Forks. Although with its low-pitched roof it seems to reflect either French-Canadian or Scandanavian design, this cabin would look at home almost anywhere in the United States or Canada, so naturally does it blend in with its surrounding. *Photograph courtesy Ronald Woodall*

STABLE

Calder, Saskatchewan

The hip roof on this lovely farm building in Calder, Saskatchewan, points to its Ukrainian origins. Ends of interior wall logs, carefully fitted into the exterior walls, are reminiscent of the seventeenth-century Swedish granary in Greenwich, New Jersey, pictured on pages 155-56. Of course, since Russia inherited the concept of building with logs from the Swedes of Viking times, the similarity between log structures built by the Swedes in the United States and the Russians in Canada is not surprising. *Photograph courtesy Ronald Woodall*

The Log Cabin Revival

It is not too surprising, in this day of rebellion against the sameness brought by modern technology and an affluent society, that log cabin building is undergoing a sort of revival. Some people, many of whom make their living in quite sophisticated ways far removed from farming in the forest, are actually cutting their own logs with a felling ax and crosscut saw, squaring the logs with broadax, smoothing the floor puncheons with a

While hunting in Alaska several years ago Rankin Smith, owner of the Atlanta Falcons football team, was intrigued by the log hunting lodge where he stayed. Later he engaged Mr. Doellefeld, its builder, to come to Atlanta and erect this magnificent weekend retreat on the banks of the Chattahoochee River some thirty miles north of Atlanta. The construction, of longleaf pine logs shipped from southern Georgia, took about three years and at a cost that ran well into six figures. A combination of elegance and simplicity, the Smith House is the ultimate in log constructions and a fine example of how the traditional American log cabin can be adapted to twentieth-century use and enjoyment.

A contemporary prefabricated log house sold unassembled. Although it retains the charm of horizontal logs, it lacks the warmth and texture of logs hewn by the builder himself. All of the logs in this house have been turned to the same diameter. Each log is channeled down its length on the underside to create a snug fit on the log beneath it. Also, each log is slotted top and bottom so that thin splines may be inserted to substitute for chinking.

In 1936, during the Great Depression, Peg and Bill Tyndale bought some farmland approximately ten miles outside Atlanta and decided to put up a log cabin for temporary living quarters. The logs were cut on the property, and the cabin was constructed by farmers who lived nearby. Interestingly, these farmers, residing in the vicinity of a large city a hundred years after this area of Georgia was a frontier, had all had experience putting up log utility buildings and were familiar with assembly methods for log construction. Because their log cabin was so comfortable the Tyndales decided to forgo building another house and to add on to the cabin. Mrs. Tyndale still enjoys living there, although the city has enveloped her property and extends for miles beyond it.

A corner of a prefabricated contemporary cabin.

The Smith House, despite its elegance, fits into its sylvan setting in the woods of northern Georgia quite as easily as pioneer cabins blended into the lost frontiers of America.

foot adz, and riving shingles for the roof with a froe and maul. They do this determinedly, oblivious of the availability of power tools and sawmills and the splendid paved roads that link them to modern technology in all its manifestations.

Other people are searching out old log buildings now in disarray and decay for sound logs that can be salvaged and used to build new log cabins and houses for permanent or seasonal residence. They use old logs because they have neither the time nor the skill to shape the timbers themselves, yet they appreciate the sculptural beauty to be found only in a house built of hand-hewn logs. Logs still provide marvelous natural insulation, well suited to conform with modern-day constraints upon the use of energy. Log houses can be wired, air-conditioned, heated from a central furnace, equipped with running water and the latest sanitary facilities. Such houses have an individuality not found in houses of brick and neat, sawn clapboards.

In the 1970s more and more people have become aware of log cabins. In fact, it is estimated that in 1977 alone over ten thousand log houses were built in the United States and more than three thousand in Canada.

Building a log cabin in any form is a craft calling for dedication and deep interest on the part of the builder. The activity and the concentra-

Mr. Doellefeld, the builder of the Smith House, personally barked each massive log and cut saddle notches with a foot adz. The logs fit so closely together that the barest minimum of fiberglass chinking was needed to seal the interstices between the logs. Logs were put in place with the help of a forklift.

Inside the Smith House the log cabin tradition of using material from the woods for furniture was continued. For instance, the bar is made from a single huge walnut log, the natural contours of the trunk have been retained and the surface smoothed and waxed to perfection. Barstools, all made by hand by the builder, are sections of a walnut log fitted with legs and polished. Such furniture is actually a refined version of the half-log benches and homemade log stools found in many early American backwoods cabins.

tion required provide a healthy escape from the harried workaday world. One can feel great empathy for the successful editor, for example, who fells and hews his own logs to build a mountain retreat for himself and his family. Or the young lawyer who has collected an ancient corner chisel, broadax, and foot adz to use in restoring an old cabin in which he and his bride will live.

For others not so dedicated to historical authenticity and the beauty of hand-hewn logs, there are now on the market a number of log cabin kits for building prefabricated log houses. These kits consist of the requisite number of prenotched round logs, lumber for joists and flooring, and roofing material. There are complete instructions on how to assemble the cabin. Material for a simple one-room structure sells for between five thousand and six thousand dollars. and a two- or three-story cabin kit will cost around twenty thousand dollars. While a prefabricated log house cannot compare with the beauty of the real thing, for some they can provide an easy and economical alternative. Kits are offered not only by

American firms, but also by firms in Scandinavia, where the tradition of log building began so many years ago. What follows is a by no means complete listing of some of the better-known log cabin kit manufacturers in this country:

Alpine Log Homes
Victor, Montana 59875

Alta Industries
P.O. Box 88
Halcottsville, New York 12438

L. C. Andrew
Cedar Log Home Division
South Windham, Maine 04082

Authentic Homes Corp.
Laramie, Wyoming 82070

Boyne Falls Log Homes
P.O. Box 721
Goshen, New Hampshire 03752

Carolina Log Buildings, Inc.
P.O. Box 617-M
Woodstock, Georgia 30188

Green Mountain Cabins, Inc.
Box 190 Dept. Y
Chester, Vermont 05143

Green River Trading Co.
RD 2
Millerton, New York 12546

Laurentian Log Homes
3682 Casteel Road NE
Marietta, Georgia 30060

Lindal Cedar Homes of the Southeast
1941 South Cobb Drive
Marietta, Georgia 30060

Log-N-Logs, Inc.
P.O. Box 212T
Shelburne, New York 13460

Lok-Log Homes
Gunnison, Colorado 81230

New England Log Homes, Inc.
P.O. Box 5056
Hamden, Connecticut 06518

Northeastern Log Homes, Inc.
Groton, Vermont 05016;
Kunduskeag, Maine 04450;
and
P.O. Box 7966
Louisville, Kentucky 40207

Northern Products, Inc.
Bomarc Road
Bangor, Maine 04401

Pioneer Log Homes
P.O. Box 267
Newport, New Hampshire 03773

Vermont Log Buildings, Inc.
Hartland, Vermont 05048

Ward Cabin Co.
Box 72 Y-8
Houlton, Maine 04730

Wilderness Log Homes
Route 2
Plymouth, Wisconsin 53073

Log purlins, though not functioning exactly as the purlins on an early cabin, nevertheless add authenticity and charm to the open ceiling of the Smith House. Chains in the rafters are an Alaskan innovation, intended to hold the structure together in case of earthquake.

Houses of logs have, in the 1970s, also reached a new status of luxury housing, something that would have been unheard of to our pioneer

The Smith House might be described in backwoods vernacular as a four-pen structure. The center of the interior is a large space for a billiard table with four wings, or open pens, radiating from it. One of these is for a living room with a massive fireplace, one for the bar, one for the kitchen, and one for bedrooms and baths, as designed by Mr. Smith. Log construction is so sturdy that no interior supports are required in any of these areas; this provides a spaciousness that is practically impossible to achieve within most modern houses.

Typical modern log home at the Commandant Properties at Le Chateau Montebello in Montebello, Quebec.

ancestors. There is a builder from Alaska, now living in Georgia, who specializes in designing and constructing huge houses of logs. In 1976 this specialist was called to Georgia, where he constructed a veritable mansion of logs for a prominent sportsman. The living room is designed for large and sophisticated parties, each of the three bedrooms has its own bath, and the widespread, split-shingled roof covers a game section, dining section, and commodious bar area. An eighteenth-century pioneer mother who reared thirteen children in a one-room cabin of squared logs would not believe her eyes to see the natural building material of the woods used to make such a castle, but there it sits graciously on a riverbank, a demonstration that log cabins are as adaptable as they have alway been.

In Canada, where beginning in the seventeenth century everything from homes to churches and, eventually, hotels and railroad stations has been constructed of logs, the present enthusiasm for log houses has extended into the mountains, suburbs, and resort communities. Entire vacation developments have been built almost exclusively of elegantly fitted Canadian log houses, which are often more luxurious than their U.S. counterparts. These structures, with the natural insulation afforded by logs, are able to withstand extreme changes in weather, need little maintenance and alteration over time, and are ideally suited to the harsh Canadian climate. Log houses can be economical, heat-efficient, and luxurious in detail at the same time. According to Jay Anderson of Laurentian Log Homes Ltd. in Val Morin, Quebec, the average log house costs about 25 percent less initially than a wood-frame house of comparable size, and, needless to say, the heating expenses for a log home are always considerably lower.

Although the three major Canadian manufacturers of materials for log houses, all located in Quebec, offer a number of set models for the types of houses available, the customer can choose from a variety of internal modifications—of room plans and bathroom and kitchen facilities, for instance—and can do the finishing on the interior of the house according to his own personal taste. The potential for self-expression and individuality of design attracts many people to log houses, and the major companies all provide the option of allowing the customer to build his own log house, with materials and full instructions that they supply. Can-Am Log House Ltd. of Waterloo, Quebec, featuring houses that range in price from $7,000 to $32,000, from the simplest summer cottage to an

Exterior and interior view of a modern log house built by Maisons d'Autrefois du Québec.

elegant four-bedroom structure, will deliver and construct their designs at an extra charge, an option available from the other manufacturers as well.

The career of Guy Piché of Ste.-Agathe-des-Monts, Quebec, can perhaps be viewed as an indicator of the increasing interest in log houses in Canada. Nine years after restoring his first log house in 1963, having completed the restoration of approximately two hundred typical historic Quebec log houses, M. Piché decided to go into business. Using his knowledge of ancient construction techniques and modern materials and production methods, and assisted by a staff of twenty, M. Piché and his Maisons d'Autrefois de Québec Inc. have been able to build three hundred models of historic log houses and six hundred entirely new log houses since 1972. Many of these buildings are made of logs taken from historic structures, their frames reconstructed on new sites, and quite a few belong to resort communities, like the houses at the Commandant Properties at Le Chateau Montebello in Montebello, Quebec, or the Mont Castor development in Ste.-Agathe-des-Monts, which are made up almost entirely of log houses, with standard exteriors and internal modifications of layout and personal details.

More and more people everywhere are being drawn to log cabin living, not only for the sake of tradition but also for the beauty and the practicality and the fulfillment that this traditional mode of architecture can contribute to contemporary life.

Bibliography

Angier, Bradford. *How to Build Your Home in the Woods*. Illustrated. New York: Hart Publishing Company, Inc., 1952.

Beard, Daniel Carter. *Shelters, Shacks and Shanties*, with illustrations by the author. New York: Charles Scribner's Sons, 1972.

Bruette, William Arthur. *Log Cabins and Cottages; How to Build and Furnish Them, by Practical Architects and Woodsmen*. Edited by William A. Bruette. New York: A. Bruette, 1934. (First part of this work [pp. 8–39] was published originally in 1889 under the title *Log Cabins* by William S. Wicks.)

Bucher, Robert C. "The Continental Log House." *Pennsylvania Folklife*, vol. 12, no. 4 (Summer 1962).

Bugge, Gunnar, and Christian Norborg-Schulze. *Stav og laft i Norge. (Early Wooden Architecture in Norway.)* Oslo: Byggekunst, 1969.

Clemson, Donovan. *Living with Logs: British Columbia's Log Buildings and Rail Fences*. Saanichton, B.C.: Hancock Publishers, 1974.

The Foxfire Book, No. 1: Hog dressing; log cabin building; mountain crafts and foods; planting by the signs; snake lore; hunting tales; faith healing; moonshine; and other affairs of plain living. Edited with an introduction by Eliot Wigginton. Garden City, N.Y.: Doubleday & Company, Inc., 1972.

The Foxfire Book, No. 2: Ghost stories, spring wild plant foods, spinning and weaving, midwifing, burial customs, corn shuckin's, wagon making and more affairs of plain living. Edited with an introduction by Eliot Wigginton. Garden City, N.Y.: Doubleday & Company, Inc., 1973.

The Foxfire Book, No. 3: Animal care, banjoes and dulcimers, hide tanning, summer and fall wild plant foods, butter churns, ginseng, and still more affairs of plain living. Edited with an introduction by Eliot Wigginton. Garden City, N.Y.: Anchor Press/Doubleday & Company, Inc., 1975.

The Foxfire Book, No. 4: Water systems, fiddle making, logging, gardening, sassafras tea, wood carving and further affairs of plain living. Edited with an introduction by Eliot Wigginton. Afterword by Richard M. Dorson. Garden City, N.Y.: Anchor Press/Doubleday, 1977.

Glassie, Henry. *Pattern in the Material Folk Culture of the Eastern United States.* Philadelphia: University of Pennsylvania Press, 1968.

——. "The Types of the Southern Mountain Cabin," Appendix C of Jan H. Brunvand's *The Study of American Folklore.* New York: W. W. Norton, 1968.

How to Build Your Cabin or Modern Vacation Home. (Popular Science Book.) 1964. $4.95, pb $3.50. Times Mirror Magazine.

Hunt, Ben. *How to Build and Furnish a Log Cabin: the Easy-Natural Way Using Only Hand Tools and the Woods Around You.* New York: Macmillan Publishing Company, 1974.

Hutslar, Donald A. *Log Cabin Restoration: Guidelines for the Historical Society.* American Association of State and Local History, Technical Leaflet #74, May 1974. Reprints are available for 50 cents each. For information, write the American Association of State and Local History, 1400 Eighth Avenue South, Nashville, Tennessee 37203.

Jordan, Terry G. *Texas Log Buildings.* Illustrated. Austin, Tex. & London. University of Texas Press, 1978.

Leitch, William C. *Hand-hewn: The Art of Building Your Own Cabin.* San Francisco: Chronicle Books, 1976.

Lessard, Michel, and Gilles Vilandré. *La Maison Traditionelle au Quebec.* Montreal: Les Editions de L'Homme, 1974.

Log Buildings. facs. ed. S. A. Witzel. Reprint of 1935 ed. pap. $4.00. Shorey Publishers, 110 Union St., Seattle, Washington 98101.

Mackie, B. Allan. *Building with Logs.* 6th ed., 1977. Mail order (cloth, $17.50; paper $10): P.O. Box 1205, Prince George, British Columbia V2L 4V3.

Mackie, B. Allan. *Notches of All Kinds: A Book of Timber Joinery.* Mail order: P.O. Box 1205, Prince George, British Columbia V2L 4V3.

McRaven, Charles. *Building The Hewn Log House.* Illustrated. Hallister, Mo. Mountain Publishing Service, 1978.

Mercer, Henry C. *The Origin of Log Houses in the U.S.* Illustrated. 1926. Pb, $2.00. Bucks County Historical Society.

Munger, John Warrick. *How to Build a Log Cabin*. Detroit: G. H. Munger, 1949.

Muir, Doris, editor. *Log Home Guide for Builder and Buyer*. Mail order ($6): Muir Publishing Company, Gardenvale, Quebec HOA 1BO, Canada. 1978.

Protecting Log Cabins, Rustic Work and Unseasoned Wood from Injurious Insects in Eastern United States, Farmers' Bulletin No. 2104, United States Department of Agriculture. Washington, D.C.: Government Printing Office, December 1962. For sale by the Superintendent of Documents, U.S. Government Printing Office, Washington, D.C. 20401. Price 15 cents.

Rempel, John I. *Building with Wood*. Toronto: University of Toronto Press, 1967.

Rosenberger, Jesse Leonard. *The Pennsylvania Germans*. Chicago: The University of Chicago Press, 1923.

Rutstrum, Calvin. *Wilderness Cabin*. Illustrated. 1961. $5.95. Rev. ed., 1972. Macmillan Publishing Company.

Shurtleff, Harold Robert. *The Log Cabin Myth*. Edited with an introduction by Samuel Eliot Morison. Cambridge, Mass.: Harvard University Press, 1939. A study of the early dwellings of the English colonists in North America.

Smialowski, Rudolf. *Architektura i budownictwo pasterskie w Tatrach Polskich*. Panstwowe Wydawn. Naukowe, 1959.

Thomas, James C. "The Log Houses of Kentucky." *Antiques, vol. CV, no. 4* (April 1974).

Weslager, Clinton Alfred. *The Log Cabin in America*. New Brunswick, N.J.: Rutgers University Press, 1969.

Wicks, William S. *Log Cabins: How to Build and Furnish Them*. New York: Forest and Stream Publishing Co., 1889.

Woodall, Ronald, and T.H. Watkins. *Taken by the Wind: Vanishing Architecture of the West*. Boston: New York Graphic Society, 1977. Don Mills, Ontario: General Publishing Co. Limited, 1977.

Woodall, Ronald. *Magnificent Derelicts: A Celebration of Older Buildings*. Vancouver, J.J. Douglas Publishing, 1975. Seattle: University of Washington Press, 1976.

Index

ACKNOWLEDGMENTS

This book is the result of the gratifying cooperation of many people, both here and abroad. Our sincere thanks is given to:

IN THE UNITED STATES: Alice and Carl Lindborg; Florence Griffin and her staff at the Tullie Smith House Restoration of the Atlanta Historical Society; Captain and Mrs. T. J. Bishop of Old Fort Nisqually; The Tennessee Historical Society Library; Theodosia (Sister) Moore and her mother, Mrs. Tom Christie; Steele Burden of the Louisiana Rural Life Museum; Consul General of Sweden Baron Carl-Henrik Nauckhoff; Mr. and Mrs. William P. Durst; Mr. and Mrs. William Tarwater; Thomas Bargeron of the Tifton Agrirama; Mrs. Betty Sheehan of the Ladies Hermitage Association; Tom Watson Brown and his father, Walter J. Brown; Celestine Sibley; Joseph B. Mahan of Westville; Senator and Mrs. Robert G. Dunn; the Minister of the Cherokee Methodist Church and his wife; Jere Wood and Judie Wood-Raiford; Consul General of Canada A. D. Ross; Vice Consul of Canada Alexander Graham; Charles Weatherup of the Canadian Consulate General in New York; Peggy Tyndale; David Sherman; Rankin Smith; John Burrison; Frank Kolarek; Dr. Wesley A. Westerberg and John Z. Lofgren of the Swedish American Institute; and Jean Blaylock of the Kentucky Department of Public Information.

IN SWEDEN: H. E. Ambassador Tore Tallroth; Countess Von Eckerman; Froken Anne Marie Molin of Scansen; and Herr Sven Svensson.

IN CANADA: M. R. Hodgson of Canadian Pacific; and Guy Piché of Maisons d'Autrefois du Québec, Inc. Special thanks are due to Nelson Doucet of General Publishing, who first suggested the inclusion of Canadian log buildings in our book and put us in touch with Ronald Woodall, the gifted artist who so generously contributed many of the Canadian and western photographs. Last, but certainly not least, thanks to Nancy Novogrod of Clarkson Potter, whose help with the Canadian research was invaluable.

The text of *The Log Cabin* was set by Adroit Graphic Composition Inc., New York, New York. The body type is Electra, designed by W.A. Dwiggins, the noted American type designer. The display type is Americana.
The book was printed and bound in Japan by Dai Nippon Printing Co., Ltd.,

Typography by Shari De Miskey.

Page layouts by Betty Binns Graphics.

Production supervision by Michael Fragnito and Rick Willett.

Editorial supervision by Carolyn Hart.